COUPLES
DETERMINED TO MAKE
MARRIAGE
GREAT

VISIONARY AUTHORS
JAMES AND CYNTHIA GREENE

Published by James and Cynthia Greene September 2, 2022

Address: Waldorf, Maryland
Website: https://www.marriagebuilt2last.com
Email: info@marriagebuilt2last
Phone Number: 410-403-3006
Social Media: @marriagebuilt2last

First Edition: September 2, 2022

Library of Congress Cataloging in Publication Data
Names: James and Cynthia Greene
Title: Couples Determined to Make Marriage Great
Description: First Edition. | Waldorf, Maryland
Includes bibliographical references.
Identifiers: | ISBN: 979-8-9868430-1-8

Subjects: Marriage, Family, Self-Help, Religious-Christianity

Scripture quotations are from the Holy Bible, God's Word Translation (GW), King James Version, (KJV), The Message (MSG), New International Version (NIV), and New Living Translation (NLT).

Printed in the United States of America

Contents

Acknowledgements vi

Dedication ix

Introduction x

Foreword xv

Chapter 1
When Love Comes Back Around and Friendship Turns to Forever . 1
James and Cynthia Greene

Chapter 2
We Weren't Supposed to be Here - BUT GOD 9
Louis and Tonia Bailey

Chapter 3
Redemption: God's Best is Always Better 17
Eric and Placida Braswell

Chapter 4
There is Power in the Come Together 26
Tony and Cassandra Ferguson

Chapter 5
Things That Surprised Me About Marriage 33
Reverends Darrel and Dr. Lisa M. Fiddermon

Chapter 6

Knitted Together But Not Perfect..40

Emilio and Sharon Grant

Chapter 7

A Man With A Dream, Needs A Woman With A Vision A Dream

Manifested is a Kept Promise. Embrace the Promise 49

William and Dr. Tasheka L. Green

Chapter 8

He Found A Good Thing 62

Demetrica "Meechie" Jefferis

Chapter 9

Crossing Paths to Brilliant Relationships 70

Drs. Philomena Marie Johnson and Dexter Johnson

Chapter 10

The Ministry of Reconciliation 79

Reverends Drs. Joel and Naomi Mitchell

Chapter 11

Love: Friendship Set on Fire 88

William and Larrissa Parker

Chapter 12

Keep The Enemy Out 98

Rodney and Michele Peake

Chapter 13

From the Bedroom to the Boardroom Balancing Marriage, Business

& Ministry as MarriageCEOs 107

Drs. Dwight and Deidra Roussaw

Chapter 14

Becoming The New ME To Become A Better WE 116

Fulton and Cortne' Lee Smith

Chapter 15

The Patience of A Married Couple Becoming

One Flesh! 123

Jason and Rhonda Turner

Conclusion..133

Afterword 135

About the Authors 141

Literary Works 154

Acknowledgements

God is the head of this project, and we would like to thank Him for seeing us through this vision. Without Him, we never would have taken on something so precious and sensitive. He helped orchestrate every step of the way.

I, Cynthia, would like to acknowledge my husband. I take on these large projects, and he jumps on board without knowing where it will take us. He trusts me, and he partners with me with vigor, ideas, and support. We could not have done any of this without us being in agreement and supporting one another. As we always say, "We do life together," and that includes everything!

We want to acknowledge Dr. Tasheka L. Green, our publisher, and friend. She made this process so easy and seamless. She went above and beyond the call of duty. She is a VERY busy woman, but we never felt like this project was not a priority. She was always available and willing to help. She helped cultivate and nurture everyone to make this book collaboration happen.

We want to acknowledge every author, speaker, and trainer that took time out of their busy schedule to come on the training calls. These calls were held to help, inspire, train, teach, and support our authors (and speakers) throughout this project. These individuals have been our coaches, mentors, teachers, and more throughout our entrepreneurial journey. We would especially like to thank Turiya Hodge, The Social Media Strategist, who poured into all of us to help build our businesses, not just the book project.

We want to thank our technical person Meghana Sj, The Sales Funnel Strategist, and her team from Stay Up Media; our Digital Marketer, Kathryn Oliver; our Virtual Assistant, Verni James; and our Project Manager, Christal Carter. Their expertise helped take the project to levels we could not do independently.

We would also like to acknowledge our first Mentor and Branding Coach, Trevor Otts, of Peak Performers, who gave us this idea in 2015. At the time, we did not have the full vision or feel we had the total capacity to take on a big project. Nevertheless, we wrote the plan down, kept it on our goals list, and never gave up on the idea. It was not until 2022 that we believed when the Holy Spirit told us that now was the time. We reviewed our notes, created a plan, and birthed this great book collaboration.

Dedication

This book is dedicated to COUPLES WHO LOVE THEIR SPOUSE. This book is dedicated to couples who have a great marriage and want to keep it that way!! This book is dedicated to couples who are great examples to those who are not married yet. This book is dedicated to couples seeking answers to their relationship situations. This book is dedicated to couples who love the Lord and put Him first in their marriage. This book is dedicated to everyone who believes in marriage.

Introduction

The media wants everyone to believe that all marriages end in divorce. They seem to make you think that more marriages end in divorce than stay married. Then they want you to believe that the ones who are married are not happy. The world makes you think that all couples are at home fighting and not getting along. Well, we brought together a group of couples to prove that this is absolutely not true.

We wrote this book to show the world that there are great marriages and that everyone can have one. The question is, "Are you willing to do the work?" Are you willing to do what it takes to "WIN" in your marriage? Are you ready to put in the work to "Build a Marriage Built to Last?" We firmly believe that all issues that couples have are solvable. We know that there are couples in the world who are happy, successful, prosperous, in love, and committed forever. Now we can prove it. We happen to personally know many couples who are doing outstanding in their marriages. We hang around some couples who have marriages that represent all that God designed it to be. In our next book, we will focus on the key elements God designed for marriage and how couples incorporate this into their own life story. These couples are not running around fighting and arguing. Instead, they are enjoying the one they married. For this book, we found 15 couples who are thriving (and not just surviving) in their marriages. They are thriving in their families, businesses, careers, and life. These couples are focused, they are equipped, and these *Couples Are Determined To Make Marriage Great.*

Every marriage goes through a struggle period in its lifetime. Some couples figure out how to work it out, and some give up and walk away. Which are you? Are you going to fight for your marriage (not WITH your spouse)? According to statistics by the CDC (Center for Disease Control and Prevention), divorce has gone down tremendously in the past decade. The divorce rate is 2.3 per 1,000 marriages.

Are you going through something right now and thinking about calling it quits? Are you looking for answers because you know there is a higher calling in your marriage than the problem or situation you are facing today?

We are here to tell you, DO NOT allow the world to dictate how you handle your marriage. Period! That means not your momma, daddy, sister-friend, counselor, NOBODY! Only you, your spouse, and The Lord should be the final answer to your problem and situation. There is NOTHING too hard for OUR GOD! Do you trust Him?

In this book, you will meet amazing couples who were brave enough to share their personal story with you. Each chapter outlines their marriage pain or trial and what they did to pull through. Furthermore, the couples shared their experiences as they were going through. Each story highlights a keyword they stand on in their marriage, a scripture, and a couple in the bible that they identify with in their marriage. Lastly, each couple shares what they do today to continue nurturing, growing, and having fun in their marriage.

As you read the stories in this book, we believe that you will find at least one couple that you can identify with. Our prayer is that their story will inspire you. Additionally, the stories will give you ideas on how you can take their transformational journey and learn some ways that you can make it through whatever you are going through. If you are not going through anything, but you know someone who is, get a second copy of this book and share it with him or her. Use this book as a training tool on how you can help someone else. For those of you who are not married yet, use this as a guide as to what not to do and learn what you can do if one of these situations does happen once you get married.

Use this book to help you search for the answers that you need. On the other hand, you can use it to learn what not to do when you get married. You can also use this book to pull together a group of friends to read the stories and answer the questions each couple poses. You can also use the book for marriage groups, church ministry groups, book clubs and relationship workshops, panels, and round table discussions. The intention of this book is to guide couples on what not to do in their relationship and what they can do to help them solve a related relationship problem.

This book is for married, newlyweds, engaged, and couples dating who are seriously considering marriage. The goal is to keep an open mind and learn from each, and every story told. At the same time, we pray that the couples will inspire you and help with the notion that not every couple is on the brink of divorce. This book shows that you can have the #MarriageOfYourDreams if you want a #MarriageBuilt2Last.

Now that we have the introduction out of the way, get ready for the first chapter where we, The Greene's, share the 40-Day Journey that we went through to prepare for our marriage, why we did it and what we learned.

Ephesians 6:12 (ESV), "Our fight is not against people on earth. We are fighting against the rulers and authorities and the powers of this world's darkness. We are fighting against the spiritual powers of evil in the heavenly places."

Reference
https://www.cdc.gov/nchs/fastats/marriage-divorce

Foreword

When we think about marriage, and we have been married for over 22 years, one of the crucial points is understanding and agreeing that we were doing this for life. We did not take our vows lightly. We were not playing games. It was not a thing where we joined in marriage and "hoped" it worked out. We both came into our marriage, understanding that it would be for better or worse, period. There is a certain comfort in that, so those early first arguments or disagreements when you would get frustrated or mad, there never was the thought of "this isn't working, so I'm leaving."

Is it easy? No, it is not easy. You will go through trials and tribulations, especially tribulations, but these challenges make your bond even stronger. The shared joys and pain build equitably shared experiences and make that love grow even more profound. Through marriage, you become a loving, winning team for the world to see.

In *Couples Determined to Make Marriage Great*, you will embark upon a journey of 15 amazing couples who were determined, as we were, to be a loving, winning team for the world to see. Through their love, faith, honesty, commitment, and efforts, you will see that the trials, challenges, and tribulations will never outlast your bond and strength when two become one and walk in unity and greatness.

Allison Seymour & Marc Clarke
Media and Radio Personalities

Chapter 1

When Love Comes Back Around and Friendship Turns to Forever

By
Visionary Authors James and Cynthia Greene

"Through skillful and godly Wisdom is a house (a life, a home, a family) built, and by understanding it is established [on a sound and good foundation], And by knowledge shall its chambers [of every area] be filled with all precious and pleasant riches."

Proverbs 24:3-4, AMP
#Purposed
Bible Couple ~ Jacob and Leah

James's Back Story

I knew I would be a husband when I was younger. As you know, there are no manuals on being a good husband and no instructions on how or what to do to make a marriage work. Therefore, as a child, you learn by what you see because children are visual, and all I saw was what my mother did, who was the one who raised me. All she did was work all the time to provide everything needed for a good, happy home. So, when I got married for the first time that is what I did because that is what I knew: work hard and provide for the family, which should make a happy marriage. Therefore, I worked four jobs to provide the best for my family and give them everything they needed.

What I did not realize was that my marriage was suffering. I was never home, because not only did I work all the time, but also when I had free time, I was hanging out with my friends and not my wife. I did not know how to communicate because when I did communicate, I was hard-pressed to get my point across and not listen to what she had to say. I also did not know how to nurture or cultivate the marriage. We never did anything together, except for maybe vacations now and then. These vacations were planned because I was either working or hanging out. I believed everything was fine. She had everything she needed and was provided for, so what more should she want. I thought our marriage was a seven or eight, and she believed it was a one or two.

One day when I came home from my second job, which was my day job, I got to the house. The house was empty. My wife had packed up everything, taken the children, and left. She had moved to some place else. I did not know where she might be or where my children were, and I had no idea this was coming. This led to the fact that I had a failed marriage. I was headed for a divorce and a downward spiral after she left. I did not see my children as much as I would have liked. I did not know where they lived, and I had to meet them at a neutral location. This caused great heartache, and things just started getting worse. I ended up having both of my cars repossessed. This caused me to start being late to work because I had to depend on public transportation. Ultimately, my house was foreclosed.

Can you imagine answering the door, and the sheriff and police are there with a moving van? The movers packed up the rest of my things and moved them to a storage facility, where I had 30 days to retrieve my items or they would be sold. The sheriff put a padlock on my door and left. I was left sitting on the front steps of what once was my home, with no place to go and no place to live. To top it all off, I lost my main job because the company I was working for went out of business. I lost my second job. That job was located in the suburbs and there was no public transportation that went to that location. My third job, a weekend job, was temporary, and that contract had ended. So now, I was left with no job, transportation, or place to live. Everything that happened to me caused me to file for Chapter 7 Bankruptcy, and I had to try to start all over again.

To be a better person and future husband, my environment had to change. Therefore, I took a job in a different city and state to get myself together and to become better. While living in this new city, I reconnected with an old friend I had met 20 years prior, and as they say, "the rest is history."

Cynthia's Back Story

Ever since I was a little girl, I dreamed of getting married in a big fairy tale wedding, wearing a big fairy tale princess dress. Welp, I unexpectedly got married while a junior in college, and for the next 20 years, I did not have a real marriage. I feel like I was tricked into getting married because the day it happened, I was told to get dressed, get in the car, and was driven out of state to a chapel. I had no idea that we were going somewhere to get married. It was not a fairy tale. It was more of a nightmare. No family. No friends. No princess dress. Not even a wedding ring! When it was time to say, "I do," I could not. No words came out of my mouth, but somehow, I said them.

Over the years, we did nothing together. We did not combine anything (not our money, friends, family, dreams), nothing. We rarely communicated, and we did not have anything in common. We did not build anything towards a future together or even our present. On paper, I created a timeline of the 25 years that we were legally married and verified that we were apart more than we were together. I felt like a single woman living in a house with a roommate.

One day, I came home from work, and he was packing. I asked him what was going on, and he said he had received his military orders to relocate to Ohio. I asked him what about us, the kids and me, and when he would tell me. He said he was going to Ohio first and then send for us later. He never did.

Lessons Learned

We both take some responsibility for what happened in our first marriage. For me, I never really got to understand my ex, who he was, what he wanted, and how to help us both to nurture and grow our marriage. Vice versa, he never truly knew me. James knew that he worked all the time, and when he was not, he was hanging out. He never took the time to nurture his marriage and be there for her. None of us knew how to communicate or "BE" married.

While dating, James and I discussed that we did not want what happened in our first marriage to happen in our second marriage (or, as we say, our "final" marriage). We decided we needed to put in the work beforehand but were not sure how. So what did we do to ensure we built a marriage that would lead to SUCCESS? We prayed and prayed, and asked God how do we do marriage His way, the way He determined in His word. We wanted to know how to have a marriage the way He created it to be before the beginning of time. We prayed to God to show us how to do marriage the right way. One day during my prayer time, God told me (Cynthia) that He wanted James and me to take 40 days and study His word. That is when the journey began.

The Journey

God specifically told us to take a 40-day journey with Him, our Lord, our God, and our Savior. We looked at the calendar and decided to begin the 40 days before our wedding date. James chose a scripture each day for the 40 days before our wedding day. He would call me each morning to share the day's scripture for us to read. We agreed that we would each read the scripture on our own that morning and meditate on it all day. In the evenings, we read the scripture, discussed it, and prayed together. At the same time, we did a full Daniel Fast. We read our 40th scripture, prayed our 40th prayer, and ended our 40-day fast on our wedding day, at our wedding reception. During those 40 days, we spent quality time with God. He helped us understand His design for marriage and what His marriage should look like. This journey helped us learn to read the scriptures, pray, fast, spend time together, get to know each other more intimately and spiritually, and put God at the center of everything we did. We know God wants us to consult Him, look to Him, and always put Him first. These are just a few things we learned during our 40-day journey and almost 15 years we have been married. Life, our marriage, and our journey are not about Cynthia, and it is not about James. It is about God and the purpose and vision of what He has called us to do in the earth.

The Now and Future

Since those days, we spent before our marriage, James and I have lived on the principles we learned. We never stopped praying together. We learned to talk about EVERYTHING. We learned that we love spending time together and doing almost everything together. We run errands together, clean the house, and do laundry. I cook. He washes the pots. We work in the yard together. Every week, Friday night is our date night. We do ministry together, and we have a business together. No one and nothing comes before each other or before our God. We have created a shared vision for our marriage and create shared (and individual) goals every year, both long-term and short-term. We kiss every day and say we love each other every day. We have created routines, rituals, and traditions in our marriage that keep us and those we love connected, focused, and always moving forward. We know what we want to do in our older years. We know what each other's dreams and desires are. It is nothing grandiose or out of reach. Nevertheless, we have many things that we plan to do together, and we always have something to look forward to and to keep our marriage strong. What we do in our marriage is not for everyone. You have to figure out what makes your marriage flow. What makes your marriage fun, forward moving, and successful. Our advice. Get coaching and "Get" God as the center always.

If You Build It, It Will Last.

In closing, we do not want what happened to us in our first marriage to happen to anyone else in his or her marriage. We all must be willing to learn how to communicate better with our spouses. We need to be students of our spouses and study them to get to know them on a deeper level. We need to cultivate and nurture our marriages so we can become stronger together. Being married is not all about you. It is about the two of you creating something together. You must learn to agree and include each other in all decisions made for your marriage's betterment. We believe that sacrifice leads to success. Therefore, there are times that you have to make that sacrifice in your marriage to have a successful marriage.

We chose Jacob and Leah as the couple we primarily identify within the bible. This is because we knew each other and were friends for over 20 years before we fell in love, started dating, were engaged, and then married. Jacob had to wait and work 14 years to marry the woman he truly loved. We know that God ordained our union. Our union was meant to be because 40 days before we married when we labored, we heard from God, and He taught us how to do marriage His way. We know our friendship over the years helped cultivate our persistence, patience, understanding, and devotion to one another. We help couples do the same while, at the same time, helping them increase and improve their marriage. We are in business together as Marriage Coaches. We firmly believe that God called us to do this ministry of helping other couples because we sought Him, listened to Him, studied His word on relationships, and learned how to do marriage His way. Therefore, He trusts us to help His children. He trusts us to do His will.

Questions

What will be your legacy?
What do your kids, family, and friends say about you and your marriage now and when you are no longer here?

Chapter Two

We Weren't Supposed to be Here -
BUT GOD

By
Contributing Authors Louis and Tonia Bailey

"...with all humility and gentleness, with patience, bearing with one another in love, eager to maintain the unity of the Spirit in the bond of peace."
Ephesian 4: 2-3, ESV
#Unity
Bible Couple ~ Priscilla and Aquila

Marriage is an important union. Marriage is so important that imagery and symbolism of marriage are applied to Christ and his relationship (Bridegroom & His Bride), commitment, love, and dedication to the church (body of Christ). This is reciprocated by building a personal, intimate relationship with him that includes love, trust, honor, respect, faithfulness, dedication, etc. (Ephesians 5:25-27, ESV).

When we say we were not supposed to be here, it is because many marital obstacles could have ended our marriage long ago, but God's plan included us standing strong with each other at these 34 years of marriage milestone. I (Tonia) recall a very early experience and dream encounter where a peaceful, consoling yet powerful voice spoke to me, saying I know what you will go through in your marriage but remember, I am here in it. You are not alone. God honors marriage but will you and I honor our marriage? Will it be easy? NO, but it can be worth it if you do not give up.

Our story is not that of a glamorous marriage. It is a story of two people who decided with a high level of determination that we are in it until death do us part, through the good and ugly, the glam, and the sham. Two people have to be willing to do the work or the work that you (couples) fail to do will miserably work you. Marriage is hard work! How can a man marry a woman thinking he has this? The truth is, most of us do not even know what that looks like. When I married Tonia, I had no skills in knowing how to talk or communicate with her. I was in the Army and understood how that form of communication worked, but in marriage, Army communication does not work. I was a man who kept things inside, and I feared that she would not understand me. Fast forward, I gave my life to Christ - to be saved, which was good, but I did not understand what that was all about or how it should have been as the head of my marriage.

Louis and Tonia Bailey let us get acquainted story started in April 1987 with an unplanned house visit with a former college roommate and her husband in Killeen, Texas. We spent the evening playing spades, laughing, and exchanging phone numbers. Our first date was at Wendy's. Louis received orders to be stationed in Germany for two years by October. He showed up with the news and a promise ring, and I had, to be honest, by letting him know a promise ring was not a two-year promise plan. However, we could stay in touch, and if I had not committed to someone else, we perhaps could pick up where we left off. Next, he walked me to the jewelry store to look at engagement rings. Of course, this is where he says I propose to him because I would not take his little promise ring. By November, we were engaged and planning a wedding. It was a whirlwind of passionate love and lust without real hard discussions about money, children (Louis already had 2), and I had not even met any of his family. During our premarital counseling from the Pastor, one question that he asked me went something like this, "What would you do if you saw Louis talking to another woman?" At 20 years old, what do you think I would do, Pastor? I said in my mind, but with my mouth open in shock, I thought, "Is this what you call counseling?" That counseling lasted probably less than 30 minutes, and I have no clue what was said after that question because Tonia was no longer present.

Still, our marriage story started 34 years ago, on April 9, 1988 (yes, we were engaged and married in less than 12 months). A few months later, he headed off to Germany. We both agree that having effective communication has been our biggest marriage struggle. We have had family drama and other children's drama, and I cannot talk to you about drama. A repeated cycle of us shutting down on each other and often avoiding resolving conflicts led to one of us exploding in anger or giving the other the silent treatment.

We were newlyweds, two young people (Louis, 24, and myself, 21), new babies in Christ. We spent our first 3.5 years in Stuttgart, Germany, where we learned and formed relationships with mature leaders. These mature leaders helped us to get rooted and build our faith on a solid foundation. I believe, had it not been for this beginning in our marriage, our love story might have honestly ended the first few years, BUT GOD. During our time in Germany, I remember having numerous dreams that God would use to confirm and show me our future marriage. As stated earlier, one dream I will never forget. I was bowing down, the glory of the Lord was so bright that I could not lift my head, but he comforted me with words of promises over my marriage and his blessed assurance.

Our marriage story has included many disappointments, sometimes harsh and cold words, actions toward each other, painful misunderstandings, selfishness, infertility, and infidelity.

We have been through many physical and emotional changes due to Louis' military career, with orders by the United States Army. Those changes were good in some instances, although they required us to often adjust to the demands of others:

- New church leaders
- New military unit assignment demands
- Separations due to deployments and training
- New job searches
- New school adjustments

We spent 20 years of our marriage adjusting and changing for others while neglecting each other as a couple and individuals, little by little.

Because of the Army, marriage, and kids, added in numerous deployments, the wall of separation became wider for a short time, looking more like roommates instead of a unified husband and wife. For me (Louis), everything was a mask. You stop talking to your wife, and then you begin to think other people understand you. However, that is a lie. From there, the marriage is on a downward spiral until the covers are pulled and you are exposed. In the 15th year of our marriage, it looked to be headed to a disastrous and bitter end, BUT GOD.

As a couple, we had to seek marital counseling where we learned to talk to each other instead of at each other and stop trying to get the last word or prove our point. We learned key communication skills and conflict resolution skills. However, most of them, we were good at using with others (church, work, etc.) but neglecting to give each other the same respect, courtesy, honor, and attention as instructed in I Peter 3:7. You know how we look good on the outside but torn up on the inside when the doors are closed to others.

Here is what I (Louis) did, indeed selling out to God, and what I mean by that I became intentional to read God's word, pray and ask God for wisdom (James 1:5, NIV).

Fast forward to two plus children and seven military moves later, we are still committed to "Always" (Atlantic Starr, our wedding song). Has it always been easy? NO, but our love commitment is strongly standing through it all. Our commitment was to each other's growth as a couple and yet two individuals with the common goal and determination to do marriage and love each other God's way. We intentionally carve out time for date nights (spontaneous and scheduled), being true to transparency, continually working on open communication, accepting each other's individuality, and having healthy priorities - God, family, service, and church.

As a couple, we can identify with many couples in the Bible, but we agree that the couple that we most identify with is Priscilla and Aquila (Acts 18:1-2, NIV). Why?

1. They were obedient and resilient to make the change that had happened by force and choice. The military forced us to make seven moves as a family, but it was our choice to obey and serve God no matter where the government sent us.
2. They were hospitable. Now we do not have the gift of hospitality, but if we see a need, we know how to make an offer to meet it, and membership at many churches makes us no strangers to accommodating.
3. There is the ability to adapt, be flexible and adjust to where God leads them. As I stated above, we have endured many changes. Some of the most challenging times were starting over repeatedly. We

knew the call of God was on our lives; therefore, being in church leadership, there was a level of frustration caused within us as a couple and individually. However, we felt restrained because we were not there to be legacy members. That could be a whole other book topic.

4. They were committed and determined with a hardworking mentality to their faith, serving, and marriage.

5. They were a picture of unity. A Jewish couple that put their life (reputation) on line not for just Paul, the Jew, but for Gentiles, to serve and to be disciples in the Gospel (Romans 16:3-4, NIV). The bridegroom is called to put his life on the line for his bride. They are called to walk together in unity with honor, obedience, respect, and loving commitment.

The transformation of our marriage happened when we both committed to loving each other as Christ has called us to love each other with agape love, including being brother/husband and sister/wife. We had to understand and strongly encourage engaged, committed Christian couples that you do not have a spouse or partner, but you have a brother or sister in Christ that is also your brother or sister, so be mindful of how you treat one another.

We had to look at the circle of influences we were connected to and be intentional about surrounding ourselves with those who had like-minded goals. We realized we had to be on the same side instead of fighting against each other. We had to apply the military tactics of being battle buddies by putting on the full armor of God (Ephesians 6:11-17, NIV) that strengthens not only your walk with Christ but also protects the perimeter of marriage and the home. Remembering that we are called to work together as one, as Amos 3:3 (MSG) says, "Do two people walk hand in hand if they aren't going to the same place?" Our goal is to have a marriage that first glorifies God and have a great time doing it. We have a strong sense of responsibility to counsel and mentor engaged committed couples to invest in their future by preparing for marriage and identifying the things each needs to address.

Question

Are you willing to be committed, transparent, accountable, and receptive to building a great marriage?

Chapter Three

Redemption:
God's Best is Always Better

By
Contributing Authors Eric and Placida Braswell

*"Then the elders and all the people at the gate said, "We are
witnesses. May the LORD make the woman who is coming into your
home like Rachel and Leah, who together built up the family of
Israel. May you have standing in Ephrathah and be famous in
Bethlehem."*
Ruth 4:11, NIV
#Redemption
Bible Couple ~ Boaz and Ruth

Boaz and Ruth, as individuals, have testimonies of faithfulness. Both can be seen as promise-keepers. Boaz kept his promise to be Naomi's guardian-redeemer and ultimately Ruth's husband. Ruth certainly kept her promise to Naomi. When we look at them as individuals who eventually each found favor from the Lord, we see how much more faithful God was to them. God showed them favor despite their situation or desperate circumstance than their faithfulness could have ever yielded on its own. From their lineage, our Holy Savior was born. We pray that each of our tests will bring forth a testimony that will build family and community, and ultimately the Kingdom of God will prosper.

His Test

As I look at it from the perspective of just being a male like Boaz, I can look at my life now and see how God has redeemed my life and redeemed my relationships. My marriage to Placida is my second marriage. We both were married before. I was married at 28 years old. My first wife passed away after 16 years of marriage. We have three children from that union. Even during difficult times in our marriage, I always loved studying marriage and relationships. Even after her death, I knew in my heart that I was still called to be married. I was called to be a husband. I was called to be a dad. It is one of the things that brings me the most joy in life.

The most difficult seasons in our relationship began around the 10th year of marriage. It became apparent that we had different goals and priorities. Our lives were moving in different directions as we pursued career and ministry goals. At the time, we had two children, who were our priority. The challenge was that we had very different approaches to that priority. For me, ministry was very important since I had been in ministry since my early 20s. Her priority was growing in her career and providing a better life for our family. My focus on ministry often led me to neglect my responsibilities to my wife. In addition, because of the demands of her career and education, the kids were with me most of the time. The wedge between us grew and caused strife within our marriage and family for a few years. When she got pregnant with our third child, she was diagnosed with cancer during her pregnancy. This is where the trajectory of things began to change for me in terms of finally choosing to focus on my family as my first ministry. I was truthfully struggling with choosing ministry before family. What helped was my ability to receive wise counsel when people I trusted noticed that I prioritized ministry over family before my marriage. They shared how much my wife needed me. I truly realized how selfish this was; the Lord showed me the error of my ways.

The reality of my family as my primary focus caused me to reprioritize everything. I repented to God and apologized to my wife despite my thoughts about her commitment to her career as she continued pursuing her education during her cancer treatment. She managed to do all of that while adjusting to being a mother to an infant and two older children. My goal before God was to repent, regardless of what she might be doing and whether I disagreed with her priorities or not. One of the things I realized was that God rewards faithfulness, regardless of what others do. During this time, my paradigm of ministry was beginning to shift. God began to redefine my service to Him. I was no longer subject to the same religious obligation. I began to experience a new way of loving God and my family. Serving and supporting my wife brought healing, reparation, and restoration to our marriage. I am grateful for the grace to repent, ask for forgiveness, and begin again in my marriage.

The first way I acknowledge the Lord's blessings and how He rewards faithfulness is when I look at the reward of being faithful during my first wife's illness. Our marriage had been restored. God showed me that despite my selfishness, God's hand was still on my life. I stood in faith by her side until she took her very last breath. I gave that gift not only to my first wife but also to our children.

The second way I believe that God rewarded my faithfulness is in the gift of my beautiful wife. Had I not been faithful to my first wife when she was sick on her deathbed, I do not believe that God would have rewarded me with the wife I have now in Placida. A year and a half after my first wife passed, I met Placida. Through our marriage, I have experienced a greater passion for family than I ever had in my life. While I am very grateful for my experience with my first wife, it prepared me for the ministry of family I would fully experience in my marriage to Placida. This is where God's faithfulness comes into full bloom! I remember praying very specifically about the type of woman I wanted to share my life with, spiritually, mentally, socially, and even physically. It mattered to me about how she cared for her family, how she cared about people, and how she cared about relationships. All of that was important to me. God gave me all that I asked for and even more! Her very life is a testimony of God's faithfulness.

Her Test

"I will do whatever you say," Ruth answered. So she went down to the threshing floor and did everything her mother-in-law told her to do" (Ruth 3:5-6, NIV).

There is so much about God's faithfulness to me that cannot be contained in a chapter. God has been more faithful to me than I could ever have been to myself. It is evident to me that He believes in His creation, even when the creation does not believe.

In this case, I was not a widow. My "Boaz" endured the gripping reality that the person you love is no longer present in the natural, and somehow, you must figure out how to make sense of your new normal. In my case, however, so many things about me had to die. If I am honest, on many days, I wished death on myself. It seemed the easier fate than to deal with the many ugly realities of my current state. While I was in a relationship for almost 20 years, we were only married for four of those years. Most of that time was spent with me doing things my way and hoping God would bless it. I was a good wife and mother, but everything was on my terms. My will had to die. My expectations of others had to die. The vision for my future had to die. Life as I knew it had to die.

"I assure you and most solemnly say to you unless a grain of wheat falls into the earth and dies, it remains alone [just one grain, never more]. But if it dies, it produces much grain and yields a harvest" (John 12:24, AMP).

I remember a time shortly after my ex-husband left our home, and the house was empty, yet at the same time, it was full of shame, guilt, betrayal, and rejection. The pain seemed unbearable. The silence was deafening because, in it, all I could hear were the accusations of the enemy of every failure, and the depression almost consumed my mind. I was a divorced single mother. I lost myself in the reality of that identity, which was too much to bear and seemed to discredit what I believed was my purpose. The emotional anguish spilled over into physical ailments and ultimately landed me in the hospital. I now describe this season as my threshing floor experience.

"The threshing floor is one of the most important aspects of the story of Ruth and Boaz. Their story emphasizes an undeniable need for a redeemer whom we can easily reach out to as long as we acknowledge our need." (Glory Dy)

It was in this sacred place that God was able to separate the wheat from the chaff in my life. God showed me what was valuable and what was wasteful. What I should hold onto and what I could finally release. God showed me myself on the threshing floor. God revealed so much to me during the three years from 2010 to 2013. It was during that time that I felt led to resuming my education. I pursued a graduate degree that focused on therapeutic interventions, counseling theory, the institution of marriage, and family structure from Liberty University. I have often remarked that God used my education to save my life. I found myself, my life, and so much more in the pages of the many textbooks, quite literally in The Word of God.

Fast forward to my encounter with Eric, which came out of a season of submission to God and choosing faithfulness over enmity. "The mind of the flesh [with its sinful pursuits] is actively hostile to God. It does not submit itself to God's law, since it cannot" (Romans 8:7, AMP). I was finally ready to be trusted with God's best. What is abundantly clear is that I spent almost 20 years in a relationship practicing for the real thing, which ultimately would happen suddenly in my life. I spent much of that time in disobedience, knowing the right thing to do but choosing my will and my way. Because of that willful disobedience, I know I suffered more than God's best for me would have allowed. However, He did not choose that fate. I did. God has truly redeemed that time and led me to my Boaz.

Their Testimony

Both of us realize that no one is beyond mistakes and, therefore, no one is beyond correction. "For the Lord disciplines and corrects those whom He loves" (Hebrews 12:6, AMP). It is important to note that mistakes do not disqualify you from faithfulness because you lack skills or make bad choices on your journey. God can still reward your faithfulness if you repent and self-correct your decisions and behaviors.

Marriage was the first institution that God established after creation. God cares deeply about the institution of marriage, so much so that He uses marriage as the analogy for His loving relationship with His Church. The husband's ability to serve his wife and love her as Christ loves the church and gave Himself is an honor and privilege. When this happens, the marriage is built on a strong foundation, part of Jesus Christ's blessed inheritance for His people. The extent that we both have been able to die to ourselves and yield to the counsel of the Holy Spirit, we have seen the faithfulness of God made manifest in our lives. The essential ingredient was humility. We both needed to die to our self-centered, self-seeking ways and confess our need for the Redeemer. Coming out of agreement with our sinful ways and into agreement with God's way is how we can even be found faithful.

In March of 2013, God's faithfulness brought us together, and we were both able to find love again in one another. Our lessons learned from our prior marriages were an undergirding for our love for each other to be lived out responsibly and carefully. Together we have realized a greater passion and purpose for our lives.

We both knew and heard God's promise over our lives: Eric as husband and father; Placida as wife and mother. For both of us, this calling is the greatest. Even though both of us have had missteps in that process, when God makes a promise, we know Him to be a Promise-Keeper. Our goals and values were not always aligned in our prior marriages. We are now able to enjoy mostly the same goals and values. Even though we both have two very different personality types, we enjoy many of the same things. We have strong core values that are perfectly aligned. The most beautiful thing is that our goals in ministry and career are complementary, which support our love for Christ and family. The life that we live together is so rewarding. We work together, we serve together, and we play together. What we are experiencing now is the reward of getting to do the things we love the most with the person we love the most. We are so grateful for how God has rewarded our faithfulness. Likewise, Boaz was faithful to the Lord, and God rewarded his faithfulness with the wife he found in Ruth. Together we have created a life where pain intersected with purpose to provide many others with a trusted skillset and toolkit to sojourn with on their specific pathways to purpose. Through the formation of BrasWellness Group, we have been able to help many couples and individuals find their way from desperate situations to joyous reconciliation. In what areas do you need to be honest or pursue true repentance so that you can experience God's best in your marriage?

Question

What are the necessary steps that you can take to strengthen your marriage or chart your path to ensure God's best in your marriage today?

Reference

https://www.christianity.com/wiki/bible/what-was-a-threshing-floor-in-the-bible.html

Chapter 4

There is Power in the Come Together

By
Contributing Authors Tony and Cassandra Ferguson

"How truly wonderful and delightful it is to see brothers and sisters living together in sweet unity! It's as precious as the sacred scented oil flowing from the head of the high priest Aaron, dripping down upon his beard and running all the way down to the hem of his priestly robes. This harmony can be compared to the dew dripping from Mount Hermon, which flows down upon the hills of Zion. Indeed, that is where Yahweh has decreed his blessings will be found, the promise of life forevermore!"
Psalm 133, NLT
#Unity
Bible Couple ~ Ananias and Sapphira Acts 5:1-10 NLT

When the tough get going, and the devil is telling you to bail out or look for the exit sign, that is when you fight harder. Recognize there is something greater on the other side.

Cassandra and I recognize the attacks and why they came and will come. We then discuss whether we will quit, whine or fight back. After 35 years, we see a better return and invest in our family to stay and fight. We will not forfeit the blessing.

Our Bishop taught us a lesson 20 some years ago. The whole is more important than the half. Who is the whole? Your family and those depending on you to fight and make it.

There are a couple of things the enemy will try to do to divert your attention from the blessing(s). The enemy will try to make you focus more on the problem, the pain, and disappointments. Therefore, here comes the blame game. It is because of you, the economy, kids, the ministry, work, menopause, or how about me.

When you get past the stage of fault finding and playing the blame game, you begin to see who brought the attack. You know and realize there is no need to waste any more valuable time playing the blame game or fault finding. You are now ready to fight for your marriage and your legacy. How many of you know there is power in "the come together?" We are not just talking in words but the spirit. This is when things shift and align because you finally decide to put your differences aside and fight in the spirit.

You realize it is not by your power nor your might but by the Lord's Spirit, that you will get through the tough times (Zechariah 4:6). Again, there is "Power in The Come Together."

One of the verses of scriptures that became real in our marriage is Psalm 133 (NLT), which signifies unity.

How truly wonderful and delightful it is to see brothers and sisters living together in sweet unity! It's as precious as the sacred scented oil flowing from the head of the high priest Aaron, dripping down upon his beard and running all the way down to the hem of his priestly robes. This harmony can be compared to the dew dripping from Mount Hermon, which flows down upon the hills of Zion. Indeed, that is where Yahweh has decreed his blessings will be found, the promise of life forevermore!

Through this verse, we begin to see the power of agreement in the spirit versus division and disagreement in the flesh. We love how the Blue Letter Bible breaks Psalm 133 down. It talks about the blessed unity of God's people. Starting with the word behold, meaning; take notice, what follows after this is important. Unity reflects God's heart and purpose. It is pleasant because it makes life together as God's people so much more enjoyable than a season of arguing. Unity is such a remarkable blessing because it is both good and pleasant. God commands the blessing of unity.

We can also look at a couple in the Bible that agreed about their finances but lied to God about them. That is Ananias and Sapphira. They sold their possession and only gave a portion of what they agreed to offer God. The Bible says they kept back, which in the Greek it means misappropriate pure deceit. Sapphira was fully aware and played a major role in the deception.

Peter asked Ananias, "Why has satan filled your heart to lie to the Holy Spirit, and you kept some of the money for yourself?" Ananias could not take the confrontation or rebuke, so he dropped dead. Now here comes Sapphira about three hours later, not knowing what happened. Peter now confronts her, "Was this the price you and your husband received for your land?" "Yes," she replied, "That was the price." Peter asked, "How could the two of you even think of conspiring to test the Spirit of the Lord like this?" Peter told her she was about to be carried out too. Instantly, she fell to the floor and died.

Therefore, the truth is do not lie to one another or God about your finances. God is all-knowing "El Shaddai;" he already knows what you have, so do not test him.

We both understood the commandment, and we knew we had to come together in unity. We agreed on the problem and the solution. Yes, the problem and the solution. This is a counterattack to keep pride from slipping in. It does not matter who created the mess. We both are taking ownership and working it out together. Real deliverance comes from living up to your mistakes and truth. Always keep the main thing the main thing.

Now that the victory stage has been set let us talk about our biggest battle, finances. Often and still at times, we do not see eye-to-eye or heart-to-heart about finances. Cassandra, the risk taker, jumps-in and asks questions later. Tony, I am going to hold a dollar until it becomes a halo and hold it some more unless there is a sale on Nike tennis shoes. Yes, there are times we saw money very differently but not when it came to God receiving his first, family, business needs, and building generational wealth.

Cassandra has over 25 years plus of financial training and teaching. Even though she liked to spend time with the finances, I often had to trust her wisdom and experience over my fears of being without. During 2008 to 2009, we owed a mortgage and processing company. We were beginning to do well in business. Cassandra was sometimes depositing checks for $30,000 into the business account.

Then the worst morning in a mortgage broker's life happened. The FEDS shut down operations for many mortgage companies because of predatory lending. This type of lending is considered an unethical practice during the loan origination process. Many banks were creating and underwriting unfair, deceptive, and fraudulent loans to make more money. The FEDS decided to shut it down in September 2008 and take over the banks. It was the worst day for many in the industry. The biggest question was, "How are we going to make it?" At that moment, we had to make a business decision and close our mortgage brokerage company.

Therefore, closing the company resulted in a loss of income. We now look at ways we can keep from losing things. After that, it took about five to eight years to bounce back and recoup our losses. We had cars repossessed, almost lost our home to foreclosure, and began to be in a very dark place of despair.

Even though all this was happening, we still came together in unity. We once moved out of our house hoping to get a renter. It fell through after we had moved out and rented another place. We let the house sit empty for a year, thinking the bank would take it. One day Cassandra decided to ride through the neighborhood. As she was riding, all of a sudden, the mortgage company called and said they wanted to speak about our home and see how they could help us to save it. That was nobody but God. God had spoken to us both saying it was time to go back home, and this time do not let the grasshopper run you out of the land I gave you. We both agreed and went back without knowing what would be next.

We are now back in the house and moved in. We both agree that God is going to perform a miracle. At that time, we read the story of Zerubbabel in Zechariah 4. In this story, the Lord said that building of the temple would not be by his own strength but by the might of the Lord. Furthermore, nothing will stand in His way when He sets that final stone of the temple. He shouted, "Grace, Grace to it!" Therefore, for every foreclosure letter we got, we held it up to God and shouted "Grace, Grace to it."

Then the miracle happened. We received the call in which we had been awaiting. The mortgage company called and said they modified our loan, giving us a 2% interest rate and knocking $296,000 off our principal. See, God knew the bubble would burst in the mortgage industry. That day in September took us by surprise, but it did not take God by surprise. The real miracle was coming together as husband and wife and agreeing on God's promise. This miracle strengthened our faith and taught us never to doubt God again. We now come together in prayer about everything. We have witnessed God doing miracles after miracles. God saved our daughter from a deadly car accident without a scratch. God held back the rain for events, healed our family members, and sent financial breakthroughs after financial breakthroughs. There is truly power in the come together.

Here is a quick formula to keep you one in your finances.

1. Identify the problem
2. Pray for a solution/strategy
3. Put your pride down and work the plan together
4. Celebrate

Question

How many of you know there is power in "the come together?"

Chapter 5

Things That Surprised Me About Marriage

By
Contributing Authors
Reverends Darrel and Dr. Lisa M. Fiddermon

"My grace is sufficient for you, for power is made perfect in weakness." So I will boast all the more gladly of my weaknesses, so that the power of Christ may dwell in me."
2 Corinthians 12:9, NRSV
#Forgiveness
Bible Couple ~ Priscilla and Aquila

The timing for getting married does not need to be long.

I met my husband, Darrel, at a Thanksgiving dinner hosted by mutual friends. After years of working as a Customer Service Executive, I realized God was calling me into full-time ministry. I was a 31-year-old seminary student working part-time at a Gospel bookstore. He was a 36-year-old Informational Technology (IT) specialist well established working with a large law firm and still exploring his call to ministry. He had his own apartment, and I had given up my apartment to move in with a friend from church while in school. Most of our families lived several miles away, and we did not have plans for the holiday. Therefore, we accepted this invitation from our mutual friends. Neither of us noticed each other seriously on that Thanksgiving, but our paths kept crossing at different church-related activities after we met.

Meanwhile, I remembered words of wisdom from a mentor who had been married for 50-plus years. Her words have transcended time; I still quote them today to other single women interested in getting married. She said, "Honey when you pray for a husband, pray that he recognizes you when he sees you." As I prayed for a husband, I could feel my inner clock ticking, letting me know my time was getting short. Yet, I continued to live my life with normalcy, not knowing that my future husband would someday single me out in a room full of strangers. Four months had passed since Thanksgiving, and we were attending a banquet on a cool spring evening. I wore my favorite white dress with gold buttons and a ruffled collar. That night, he saw me from across the room and decided to ask me out on a date. I agreed. To this day, more than 25 years ago, he still remembers that dress and said there was something different about how I looked that night.

We dated several times for three to four months after that banquet. We ate at various restaurants, caught an Alvin Ailey production, enjoyed walks in the park, and explored many of Washington, DC's musical sights and sounds. We were often engaged in endless conversations on the phone. Once, we talked all night until the break of dawn. We had become very close friends. Darrel was finding peace with a finalized divorce, and I was checking my "husband-to-be" list. Then one night, while we were dancing, I realized that I loved this man and could not imagine my life without him. It was also the first time we confessed our love to each other. Weeks later, we were meeting our friends for the Fourth of July celebration at the National Mall. I was resting my eyes while seated on the sofa in his apartment and waiting for him to get dressed. When my eyes flew open, I found him kneeling with a marriage proposal to me. My answer was a definite yes. I said yes because I loved him. I said yes because I loved being in his company. I loved his intellect and our deep conversations. I loved that he respected me and understood me. I loved him because he was a man of faith. We celebrated our engagement with beautiful fireworks. After a few months of premarital counseling and a year's engagement, we celebrated again with fireworks. We were married on June 14, 1997, and we later discovered it was Flag Day, which ended with a firework show on our honeymoon in Baltimore, Maryland.

A marriage can be struggling and still be strong.

I always thought that marriages that struggle would ultimately end in divorce because of the way I saw my parents struggling. Darrel and I both had parents who ended their marriage in divorce. Yet, we were intentional about not repeating the same mistakes we thought our parents made. We decided that we would not become our parents. We believe that "marriage is what **we** make it," which means **we** make the final decisions about what works for us and not compare our marriage to others. We are not the couple that dresses alike or is openly affectionate and hopelessly romantic, but we often finish each other's sentences and have affectionate names for each other. In my research and experience, I have learned that most couples struggle with communication, childrearing, career development, intimacy, and finances.

Financial struggles have always been challenging throughout our marriage for both of us. We prolonged either unemployment for several months or disagreements on how to spend our incomes. Our biggest struggle began in our 20th year of marriage. We were serving in ministry together in a small, aging congregation. I was full-time salaried with the church, and Darrel was bi-vocational. We were the first African Americans to serve as Lead Pastors in the 70-year history of this church. As a clergy couple, we had big plans to help revive the church and engage the community. The congregation welcomed some of these plans, but we still received passive support. Although we accomplished wonderful things together, it was not nearly as much as we had hoped. My income from the church was often unpredictable. There were several times when I went a week without pay. Darrel was a very well trained and experienced IT professional who had been overlooked for at least three permanent employment positions. He spent a lot of time working for Uber, but our annual income had still dropped by $50,000. Our oldest daughter Sakile' was applying to colleges, and senior year high school expenses were piling up. Our youngest son Darrel Judah played basketball in sports leagues to help secure college scholarships, and costs were attached to that.

Meanwhile, we were behind with our mortgage to the brink of foreclosure. We quickly learned where the local food distributions were located, and I learned how to grocery shop at the Dollar Store. Darrel and I were barely talking because we had so much tension. We tried to keep our connection strong, but the stress we were under was indescribable.

As a family, our well-being was in trouble. Anxiety, depression, disappointment, and disillusionment were unavoidable. We prayed consistently, saw a good therapist, reinforced positive affirmations, leaned into supportive friendships, and kept a sense of humor. This contributed to how our marriage remained strong and survived this challenging time. By the grace of God, we did not lose our home and could maintain most of our middle-class lifestyle. Similar to God's word through the Apostle Paul, these experiences have taught me that God's power is truly made perfect in all our weaknesses. (2 Corinthians 12:9, NRSV).

So how did these experiences make our marriage stronger and our lives better? We became even more committed to finding solutions, more appreciative of each other, more mindful of God's love and provision for us, and now inspired to share more wisdom from our struggles to encourage other individuals and couples.

Forgiveness in marriage requires more effort than expected.

I have lost count of the many times Darrel and I have had to forgive one another. Forgiveness for disappointments and hurts I have imposed and what was imposed on me. I am not so surprised by how hard forgiveness can be but more surprised by how easy resentfulness can set in even when I thought I had forgiven.

For this reason, I have found that I often need to take time to forgive myself. I work hard at forgiving myself for wrongly taking responsibility for things that are not in my control. I have given my own permission to forgive myself for believing lies over the truth and for choosing fear over faith. I had to forgive myself for questioning my purpose, not being perfect, not feeling and living my best self, and apologizing for too many things.

Forgiving the mistakes, I have made on job applications, on interviews, and at church as a Pastor, for not giving myself enough credit, for being too critical, and for not being understanding enough with others and myself.

I learned that forgiveness allows me to be free to control what is in my control. To give myself the credit I deserve and to be more accepting of myself. To pursue my purpose, to feel and live my best self. To live in truth, to choose faith over fear, and learn to enjoy God's presence in my life and marriage. For me (us), staying intentional in forgiving is a part of our marriage strategy.

So, what are some practical things we do to keep our marriage strong, exciting, growing, and prospering? We perform kind gestures like cooking a favorite meal, picking up extra chores, or giving each other space and time to relax after a stressful day. We take random getaways. We pray for each other. We talk and reminisce about our life together to reconnect and inspire future activities. We hold hands. We accommodate each other's needs by being flexible and making changes as they occur. We say the words "I love you" every day. We are intentional about doing all of these things and more. We stand on a few principles in our marriage, but the most important one is staying intentional.

Darrel and I are a unique couple like Priscilla and Aquila in Acts 18:24-26 (New Revised Standard Version). Priscilla and Aquila intentionally worked together in ministry for the good of God's kingdom. They were intentional and faithful in sharing the message of the good news of Jesus Christ to as many people as possible. They were tentmakers who were just as intentional about patching holes and repairing tears as they were about helping to mend people's lives in crisis. They were also a couple who intentionally kept their love strong and stayed together throughout life's challenges in their marriage.

Question

What practical ways can you keep love strong, work together for better solutions, and stay intentional in your marriage?

Chapter 6

Knitted Together, But Not Perfect

By
Contributing Authors Emilio and Sharon Grant

"Two are better than one because they have a good reward for their efforts. For if either fall, his companion can lift him up; but pity the one who falls without another to lift him up. Also, if two lie down together, they can keep warm; but how can one person alone keep warm? And if someone overpowers one person, two can resist him. A cord of three strands is not easily broken."
Ecclesiastes 4:9-12, CSB
#Commitment
Bible Couple ~ Joseph and Mary

I was devastated and horrified, not prepared for what was about to happen in our life. As I approached our home, I saw police and unmarked cars lined along the side of the street of our home. My son, Jonathan, 17 years of age at the time, grabbed his head and bent over as if in a fetal position, started yelling repeatedly and crying, "Mom, I messed up, I'm sorry!" I screamed in terror, "What did you do? You better tell me before we get out of this car!" This was my attempt to try to "get myself together" before I entered our home. All he repeated was, "I messed up, Mama, I'm sorry!"

As our son left our home, he hugged me and said, "Mama, don't worry, I'll be okay, call my dad." He hugged me and was escorted out of the house in handcuffs. I was overwhelmed with so many emotions that I could not name or describe them. One of the police officers said, "Ma'am do you believe in God?" I replied, "Yes!" He said, "Then pray." His statement began yet another spiritual episode in our faith journey.

I contacted Emilio via the phone to come home because Jonathan had been arrested. Emilio recounted the many conversations where he discussed with Jonathan, that his actions would have consequences that would affect him and others as he drove home. When Emilio arrived home, I shared the details, as I knew them. Emilio appeared emotionless as we talked. He shared that once he was alone, anger kicked in as he sat alone with his thoughts. He was angry with Jonathan, then, but later, he expressed anger at himself.

I had to go to teach my first collegiate course, Family Therapy, at a local Christian College the evening of my son's arrest. I considered not going, but I felt an inner commitment or pulling to honor that obligation. I felt focused and peaceful while teaching the students that night. It was only by the grace of God and the supernatural filling of the Holy Spirit that allowed me to escape my devastation and emotional pain long enough to be present with the students and teach the class.

When I asked my husband, Emilio, where to begin when writing this chapter, he replied, "The beginning." I laughed and replied, "I don't think we have enough pages for that!" Emilio and I have been married for 14 years. When we married, Jonathan was nine years of age. We dated for a year before marriage. Emilio was away serving a tour in Qatar when his sister introduced us. We talked on the phone and emailed each other for about four months before he returned home to the states. We would talk on the phone until one or both fell asleep! We had the luxury of genuinely getting to know each other without the pressures or distractions of in person dating. We asked each other tough but pertinent questions about our past, including upbringing, earlier marriages, future goals, values and beliefs, future marriage, children, and current circumstances. Because of this, we both felt like we knew each other already when we met for the first time in person at his welcome home party.

I introduced Jonathan, to Emilio about six months into our dating relationship. We included John's biological father because we expected potential loyalty issues and wanted to be proactive. His father supported and encouraged John in our relationship, future marriage, and new family. Was his biological father's minor involvement necessary? No, but was it helpful and significant? Yes!

This paved the way for Emilio and Jonathan's, father to discuss directly any challenges concerning Jonathan.

Emilio and I received pre-marital counseling in a group setting at our local church. You do not know what you do not know. Had we known what we know now, we would have sought individual couples counseling to address our unique situation(s). We believe we would have better understood what "our" potential marital challenges could have been. I believe premarital counseling needs to address particular circumstances, such as blended families. It needs to be tailored to the specific couple and their needs.

We moved to Warner Robins, Georgia, where Emilio was stationed and concluded his 25 years of service in the United States Air Force. Emilio was new to the blended family situation, while I was not. In my earlier marriage to Jonathan's father, we were also a blended family. Emilio went from a single man, responsible for himself only, to a "ready-made family." He has teased me over the years that he always knew from day one that Jonathan and I were a package deal, and he accepted us.

The transition was a little difficult during our time in Warner Robbins as Jonathan began having behavioral problems in school, a new and stressful job for me being on call at a Substance Abuse Residential Program, in addition to a new baby, Jared. Emilio had not changed his single man work habits because he continued to work late, coming home late. Even when I had Jared, he arrived just in time as the doctors took me back for delivery. He was still at work when his unit commander told him to leave and come to the hospital. Nevertheless, I was pleased to see him when he arrived.

One of Emilio's top values is respect. He honored and respected his mother and expected Jonathan to do the same. When he saw Jonathan being disrespectful, he would interject to defend me. This was an honorable act, but because of my faulty beliefs from my experience dating back to childhood about blended families, I felt he was too hard on Jonathan. This caused conflict between Emilio and me. This conflict would continue throughout our marriage until Jonathan's incarceration.

Our difference of opinion on how things should be done was a dividing force and prevented us from approaching our blended family as a partnership. Instead, Emilio was seen as an outsider and was falsely accused of not caring for Jonathan, as he should. My unspoken expectations led to frustrations when Emilio did not respond as I felt he should.

Emilio expressed that he did not feel like an outsider. He shared that he did not communicate his feelings openly because he thought doing so would cause more conflict. He said that he fell short on one of his main duties as a husband, to communicate in full transparency about his observations over the years. He felt he was silent when he needed to intervene and speak up despite my objections.

We moved again once Emilio retired to be closer to family. We found a church home and volunteered in church ministries. We continued to experience parenting challenges. We had about three significant situations, including earlier parenting challenges, which prompted me to suggest and consider divorce or living separately. I felt hopeless and very torn. Emilio reiterated that he was not going anywhere, and he was committed. We both were previously married and desperately wanted our marriage to work. After all, we loved each other! The thought of leaving quickly dissipated because of my love for Emilio and commitment to him and our family. We realized that the issue was not our child. The real problem was we did not have the emotional bandwidth, parenting, or relationship skills necessary to maneuver the often-rough terrain of a blended family. Nevertheless, because of our commitment, we persevered.

Leading up to Jonathan's arrest, several things that can only be explained as divinely inspired forewarned us of what was to come. My last warning to him was, whatever you are doing would become known. You had better stop it now. Not much time passed before his arrest.

Jonathan was sentenced to serve eight years in prison. This was a death sentence to us. We do not make light of those families who have loved ones serving life in prison or have been sentenced to the death penalty. My limited perspective then was, my 17-year-old son serving time with grown men is never going to get out! He will not make it out!

This was indeed a test of our faith and commitment to trust God. God had told me that as I do what he has called me to do; he will take care of Jonathan. I could not understand in my logical brain how allowing this to happen was taking care of him. Faith is not logical. It is trusting God, despite what we see happening in the natural that he has a plan and a purpose, working things out for our best.

It was as if I was just going through the motions, taking care of what was needed from me but not living a joyful life. It was as if we were incarcerated with our son for the first couple of years. Emilio and I experienced the same emotions, anger, sadness, disappointment, frustration, concern, guilt, blame, shame, and embarrassment. We struggled with how this happened to our family. The shame and embarrassment affected me for a long time and prevented me from networking and pursuing business-related opportunities. God reminded me to trust him in all things and have faith.

Emilio began reading the Bible more and nurtured his relationship with God. He said his anger was "getting the best of him." His heart has since been healed of the anger, which freed him to connect and relate to Jonathan in a way he never had. He said his encounter with God at church helped him to release the blame he had placed on himself.

Over these years, we have seen definite positive changes and growth in Jonathan's view of himself and the situation. He accepts responsibility for his decision-making. He said he does not blame anyone but himself. He has reconciled his thoughts and feelings about our blended family. He is 23 now, and the lenses through which he sees things have expanded and are more apparent.

We arrived at the stage of acceptance of reality. The acceptance of our situation along our journey, growing more in our faith and relationship with God. We have come to believe that God will use all our experiences (good and bad) for His glory and our testimony if we are willing to share the trials we have endured with others. We no longer felt isolated without great support from family, close friends, and church family. We prayed consistently for his divine protection and transformation, which God has honored. The prayer of a righteous person is very powerful in its effect.

As we presented ourselves to God, hurt and broken, and allowed him to heal our hearts, we no longer lived in shame or guilt and experienced true freedom. Emilio and I became small group leaders through our local church. Facilitating the small group using the book, *One Family Under God* by Tony Evans gave us a new purpose in the marriage of our roles, responsibilities, and how to support each other. The small groups allowed us to share with other believers transparently. Our focus was no longer "poor us," but we realized we had a greater purpose: to help other couples by sharing our marriage experiences. Another small group we facilitated using the book, *The Circle Maker* by Mark Batterson was impactful because we sharpened our warfare weapon of prayer. We understood that we were planting seeds that would eventually bear fruit and manifest blessings in the future. After about a year of praying to God and asking Emilio to join me in my coaching and counseling business to work with couples, he agreed. We both are Prepare-Enrich Certified Facilitators and coach couples through our Enrich Marriage Coaching Program for married couples. We are deep in the summer season of our marriage in which we are comfortable with each other, feel secure, enjoy life, and support one another. We are also in early springtime, in which we are open with each other in full transparency, filled with hope and anticipation.

The Bible couple that resonates with us is Joseph and Mary. Their story reminds us that commitment will last through the good times and the troubled times. They trusted God despite the unknown. Love can grow stronger through our difficulties.

Looking back over our marriage experiences, we can see God's handiwork knitting us together for His use and glory.

Question

What is one action you can take that shows commitment to your marriage?

Chapter 7

A Man With A Dream, Needs A Woman With A Vision A Dream Manifested is a Kept Promise. Embrace the Promise

By
Contributing Authors
William and Dr. Tasheka L. Green

"Her husband has full confidence in her and lacks nothing of value. She brings him good, not harm, all the days of her life."
Proverbs 31:11-12, NIV
#Promise
Bible Couple ~ The Shunammite Woman and Her Husband

W hat do you do when what you have been promised no longer brings forth life? This could be anything from what you hoped for, dreamed of, believed in, or aspired to become. When you heard the promise, saw the promise, embraced the promise, gave birth to the promise, and it was taken away from you. What do you do?

A promise is a declaration or assurance that one will do a particular thing or that a particular thing will happen. As a verb, a promise means to commit oneself by a promise to do or give. A promise is sacred and a verbal commitment that is not meant to be broken.

Every promise over your life is true and full of life—it rewires how we think and unites our hearts with God, others, and ourselves. For it is not your promises but the promises God gave to you.

Promises are usually hard because they require us to step outside of our norm, not to think outside of the box, but to throw the box away, be in the very face of fear, but go about it anyway with courage, to walk some places alone, and to have faith that never gives up.

Always be known as one who dares to believe the impossible is possible with God. Everything God has promised for you, He is going to do it. The only distance between what God has said and the promises you seek is your ability to surrender your will and be obedient to God's plan and timing.

How big is your promise? What has God promised you? Is life over, or has it just begun?

Let us recall the story of the Shunammite woman in 2 Kings 4:8-36. We do not know the name of the Shunammite woman and her husband, but we know the story of what they did and its extraordinary impact on their lives and others. So often, we are caught up in names, titles, and positions and we introduce ourselves first, with what we do rather than who we are. It is not what you do that matters but who you are and how you share God's love with everyone who passes your way.

Elisha was passing through Shunem, and every time he went through, he stopped at the Shunammite woman's home to eat. She was so confident Elisha was a holy man that she said to her husband, "Let's make a small room on the roof and put in it a bed and a table, a chair and a lamp for him. Then he can stay there whenever he comes to us" (2 Kings 4:10, NIV). Her husband never questioned or doubted her. "Her husband has full confidence in her and lacks nothing of value. She brings him good, not harm, all the days of her life" (Proverbs 31:11-12, NIV). Therefore, the Shunammite woman made Elisha a place to rest, commune with God, get instructions, and speak for God by preparing a small room with a bed, table, chair, and lamp.

The Shunammite woman was a well-to-do woman, a woman of virtue, wise, hospitable, nurturer, and served others and her family. Her husband was a hard worker, cared for his family, found trust and value in his wife, and created the conditions so she could be who God created her to be.

"In the beginning, was the Word, and the Word was with God, and the Word was God" (John 1:1, KJV). From the foundations of the Earth, all we ever had was a word. In the story of the Shunammite woman and her husband, Elisha passed by and had a word for them both. From that word, the husband created, and the Shunammite woman conceived. It was all because of the plan of God, His purpose that needed to be fulfilled, and the promise of God that was on their life.

In the beginning, when God created man and woman, Adam's responsibility was to create, and Eve's responsibility was to conceive. The word was already given to the Shunammite woman and her husband. Therefore, it had to be manifested through them by giving birth to the promise. Nevertheless, when asked what she needed, the Shunammite woman responded, "Nothing. I am secure and satisfied with my family" (2 Kings 4:16, MSG). However, the gift of God in Elisha knew the Shunammite woman and her husband had a promise from God. Elisha conferred with his servant, and Gehazi said, "Well, she has no son, and her husband is an old man" (2 Kings 4:14, MSG). At this point, Elisha brought forth a word of life, "About this time next year," Elisha said, "you will hold a son in your arms" (2 Kings 4:16, NIV).

However, even though the Shunammite woman and her husband received the word from Elisha, she did not want to be disappointed, discouraged, or discontent. The Shunammite woman replied, "O my master, O Holy Man," she said, "don't play games with me, teasing me with such fantasies!" (2 Kings 4:16, MSG).

And God remembered the Shunammite woman and her husband. The story continues and the woman became pregnant, and the next year about that same time, she gave birth to a son, just as Elisha had told her. The child grew, and one day he went out to his father, who was with the reapers. He said to his father, "My head! My head!" His father told a servant, "Carry him to his mother." After the servant had lifted him up and carried him to his mother, the boy sat on her lap until noon, and then he died. She went up and laid him on the bed of the man of God, then shut the door and went out" (2 Kings 4:17-21, NIV).

When the husband said, "Carry him to his mother," he knew that this woman, his wife, was his help meet, his rib, which the Lord God had taken from man, made he a woman, and brought her unto the man, bone of his bones, and flesh of his flesh (Genesis 2:18, 22-23, KJV). He knew that as his rib, she was a protector of dreams, a supporter of hopes. This life-giver would breathe life and love you to a place called victory. The husband trusted the nurturing capability of his wife, and she trusted the word that God gave through Elisha. What God had promised, died right in front of her. What do you do when your dreams and visions fade away right before you?

As the story proceeds, the Shunammite woman lays the son, the promise, on Elisha's bed. The bed she had prepared. She shut the door and looked for Elisha (Verse 21). She was a very wise woman and did not want to distress her husband's emotions by informing him about their son. She did not want to tell him the promise was dead. Therefore, she asked her husband to send one of the servants and a donkey, so she could go to the man of God quickly and return (Verse 22). At this moment, the husband asks a question, "Why go to him today?" (Verse 23). She spoke to him and said, "It shall be well" (Verse

23). The Shunammite woman knew that she and her husband had a promise, and their promise shall live.

Therefore, the Shunammite woman and the servant set out for Elisha, informing the servant not to slow down unless I tell you (Verse 24). When Elisha saw her from a distance, he sent Gehazi to meet her, and he asked if she was well, if her husband was well, and if her child was well (Verses 25-26). The Shunammite woman told Gehazi, "It is well" (Verse 26). This may have been one of the heaviest family afflictions that could transpire for her and her husband, but she had great faith in knowing "It is well." She told Gehazi, "It is well," because he did not have her answer. She wanted the one who spoke the word; she wanted the promise. When she reached Elisha, she grabbed his feet. Elisha could see she was in great distress but did not know why (Verse 27). Gehazi even attempted to pull her away from Elisha, but Elisha said to leave her alone (Verse 27). The Shunammite woman spoke up and said, "Did I ask for a son, master? Didn't I tell you, don't tease me with false hopes?" (Verse 28).

At this moment, Elisha instructed Gehazi to restore the child (Verse 29). Nevertheless, the Shunammite woman was adamant that she was not leaving without Elisha (Verse 30). Gehazi went ahead of them both. When Gehazi arrived at the house, he entered the room and did as Elisha instructed, but the son's condition did not change (Verse 31). Gehazi went back to meet Elisha and told him what had happened. Elisha arrived at the house and saw the son; the promise was dead. He entered the room, shut the door, prayed, laid on the son, the promise, and his body grew warm (Verses 33-35). Elisha walked back and forth, got on the bed, stretched out once more, and then the boy sneezed seven times and opened his eyes

(Verse 35). When life came back into the son, the promise, Elisha called for the Shunammite woman to get her son. Before getting her son, she fell at Elisha's feet, bowed, and took her son (Verse 37).

This very child was later to become the prophet Habakkuk, whose name means embrace. The Shunammite woman and her husband embraced the promise and birthed a miracle. This is the same son, the promise, that wrote, "Then the Lord answered me and said: "Write the vision and make it plain on tablets, That he may run who reads it. For the vision is yet for an appointed time; But at the end it will speak, and it will not lie. Though it tarries, wait for it; Because it will surely come, It will not tarry" (Habakkuk 2:2- 3, NKJV).

The Shunammite woman and her husband is a story that is dear to us. Just like the two of them, we do not seek popularity; we only want purpose. We do not desire importance but only to be impactful. We only want the plan of God to be birthed out of us so that His promises will be fulfilled in us. We want to embrace the promise.

We want to make God's name great. We always want to be loyal to God's assignments and found doing His will. We want to always be in a position to bless others and a posture of worship. If we get into a place where it feels all of our faith is gone, we hope in the Lord and hold fast to the feet of the cross, the feet of Jesus. Just like the Shunammite woman held fast to Elisha's feet when she went to see him about her son, and when life was restored to him, she fell at his feet, bowed, and worshipped. We do not know the names of the Shunammite woman and her husband, but God knew their name, saw them, and rewarded them with a promise.

The purpose, plan, and promises of God are what is keeping us, sustaining us, and what we are seeking. The room she had prepared for Elisha was the same place where life would be restored to her promise. No matter what state you are in, God's plans must prevail, and His promises cannot return to Him void. "God is not human, that he should lie, not a human being, that he should change his mind. Does he speak and then not act? Does he promise and not fulfill?" (Numbers 23:19, NIV).

Within seeking God's promises, just like the Shunammite woman and her husband, we encountered several oppositions and obstacles that tried to interrupt the plan of God, snatch the purpose, and destroy the promise. "But God, who is rich in mercy, for his great love wherewith he loved us" (Ephesians 2:4, KJV). All we had and have is a word. All we had and have is God's love for us. All we had and have is to trust God. All we had and have is a promise. We held on to what God said and continued to put all our hope in Him. We had to let love wash away every disappointment, discouragement, and discontentment. We could not let disappointment, discouragement, and discontentment silence our voice. We had to pray, commune with God, get His instructions, and communicate with each other. We had to resist every distraction and focus on "Let there be."

During our 14 years of marriage, we never knew what we would encounter. All we knew was we had a promise from God. We had to embrace the promise. We had to hold onto the promise. We had to nurture the promise. We had to protect the promise. We had to believe in the promise.

We have gone through so many different seasons, but the best part is that God was, has been, and will be with us through every season. Ecclesiastes 3:1 (NIV) tells us, "To everything, there is a season and a time to every purpose under the heaven." Galatians 6:9 (NIV) also tells us, "Let us not become weary in doing good, for at the proper time we will reap a harvest if we do not give up." During some of the seasons, we faced several challenges and hardships. Life has brought us some highs and lows, the balconies and the basements. We both experienced the loss of our mothers in March of 2009 and 2010. The loss of both of our mothers birthed a foundation to carry out their legacy, give back and serve others. At one point, it appeared that life was a whirlwind, and our marriage was going in a downward spiral, resulting in no hope. However, each day, we continued to trust and believe in God and that He will change our situation, condition, and position.

Our marriage has been challenged with communication, intimacy, and financial dilemmas. There were several silent, cold, lonely, dreary days and nights. It seemed as though contentment, peace, love, and abundance were not within reach. What we were going through did not look, feel, sound, smell, or taste good. We recall when we were going through an arduous time in our lives: physically, we were exhausted; and emotionally, we were bitter. The exhaustion of the process left us fatigued, wearied, and weak. We were consumed with the process, which had depleted us of strength and energy. We barely had enough strength to get through the day. Once we arrived home, there was nothing more to do than curl up in a ball and sleep our cares away. The bitterness we carried resulted from grief, anguish, and disappointment. We painted a smile on our faces in front of people, but it faded away when we were alone. The recurring role we performed daily looked differently in front of people versus behind closed doors. This performance was not going to get us a stellar award. We could remain exhausted and bitter or become restored and better. We chose restored and better and God remembered The Greens.

We held firm to the word of God and the prophecy from our Pastor, Bishop Donald A. Wright Sr., that our marriage would not end in a divorce but would be a demonstration of God's unfailing love to help others. The questionable, silent, and isolated times in our marriage, brought forth God's word of healing and hope, which has allowed us to share healing, hope, and God's word with others. We are still here, living a purposeful life.

When life gave us lemons, and we both had lost our jobs, we did not just make lemonade; we purchased the entire lemonade stand. It birthed our businesses and the many platforms we use today to help others leverage their calling, gift, passion, and purpose to maximize their greatest potential. For 13 years, we had been in a stagnant place, a complacent state of mind, and God violently interrupted our life to show us that there is more for us. The loss of our house birthed a home of peace, joy, and love.

We overcame our challenges by maintaining our trust in God and understanding that love is a commitment to each other's victory. Love always wins, and God is perfect love. We had to create the conditions we desired, renew our minds and our commitment to God and each other, transform our thoughts, speak words of life, and then turn all of this into action. We had nothing to lose but everything to gain. We are committed to each other's victory, to the promise, and inspired by the love of God. We overcame whatever we encountered by the blood of the Lamb and the words of our testimony (Revelation 12:11, KJV). Through this, we gave birth and will continue to give birth to the promises of God.

While we were going through the process of obtaining the promise, we heard the prophecy that our marriage would not end in a divorce; rather, it would be a demonstration. That promotion would come for my husband and me, and we would walk in a place called more than enough; this process would not destroy us but bring us closer to the promise of God for our life. We heard the promise and envisioned the end, but the process of obtaining the promise seemed so dim and distant. The course God had ordered was full of events that taught us to "walk by faith and not by sight" (2 Corinthians 5:7, KJV).

As we embrace the promises of God, we value letting each other dream freely, protecting our vision, covering each other's hearts in prayer, speaking words of life over one another, nurturing each other's hopes, and giving birth to the promise. This has made our relationship and marriage stronger by standing on the promises of God and holding on to His word.

Therefore, we ask you again, "What do you do when what you have been promised no longer brings forth life?" As for my husband and me, we held on to the word, to the promise God made to us. "For no matter how many promises God has made, they are "Yes" in Christ. And so through him the "Amen" is spoken by us to the glory of God" (2 Corinthians 1:20, NIV). We did not have to understand what God was doing in our lives, but we had to trust that He would fulfill every promise to us. "Trust in the Lord with all your heart and lean not on your own understanding; in all your ways submit to him, and he will make your paths straight" (Proverbs 3:5-6, NIV).

We encourage you to put all your trust in God and let Him be your confidence. He is the God who gives and keeps His promises. He is the God who gives and fulfills dreams. He is the God who gives and restores life. He is the God who changes seasons. He is the God who begins and completes. Put your confidence in God. Place your hope in God. It is His promise that will be fulfilled in your life. If God said it, He will perform it. "…being confident of this, that he who began a good work in you will carry it on to completion until the day of Christ Jesus" (Philippians 1:6, NIV).

God has given you a fresh vision for your future filled with courage, hope, and a promise to move forward. Regardless of what has happened and what is happening around you, God cannot break His covenant of love for you. Your future is nothing like your past. Your steps are ordered. The promise is intact, and the covenant cannot be broken. Stay focused on the promise. It is calling you and pulling you to your future. God's promises are as true as His name. God's eternal love for you moves His heart and releases the fulfilled promises. Hold on to the promise because "A dream manifested is a kept promise." God is, has, and will keep His promises to you.

Affirmations for the Journey…
The plan, purpose, and promise for our lives are safe in God.

Our promise is pulling and calling us to our future.
God's covenant with us cannot be broken.
God is keeping His promises to us.
We are a kept promise.
And God remembered (add your names).

Reflections for the Journey...

Reflect on your marriage and where you are in life.
Identify the things you are grateful for, the promises God
has made to you, the things you have already overcome,
and the things you have accomplished. Write them down,
and place the list where you can see them daily. Remind
yourself of just how amazing you are and that you are the
apples of God's eye. Let those thoughts inspire, refresh,
renew, and remind you that you are a guaranteed success
in God and the promises for your life are still alive.

Encouragement for the Journey...

Questions

What promises has God made to you and your spouse?
How are you protecting and nurturing the promise?

Chapter 8

He Found A Good Thing

By
Contributing Author Demetrica "Meechie" Jefferis

"He who finds a wife finds what is good and receives favor from the LORD."
Proverbs 18:22, NIV
#Fortified
Bible Couple ~ Elkanah and Hannah

By November 1990, I had been in the United States Air Force for 15 months. Barksdale Air Force Base, Louisiana, was my first duty station. I had been there for roughly one year and was tired of the location, my job, and trying to find LOVE. I look back on that time in my life and think how silly I was to believe that I would probably be single for the rest of my life. I was only 20 years old, for crying out loud! However, something exciting and forever life changing also occurred in November 1990, I received an assignment to Andersen Air Base, Guam. While I knew absolutely nothing about Guam, I was excited that the Air Force considered me special enough to be selected for relocation to paradise. News about my assignment could not have come at a better time. Obviously, over time I learned a lot more about Guam. The more I knew, the more excited I was to leave Shreveport-Bossier City/Barksdale and explore life in the Pacific.

In May 1991, I left Barksdale Air Force Base. After some vacation time back home in Chicago and with other relatives in Northern California, I departed for Guam on May 23, 1991. I arrived on May 24, 1991. Guam appeared to be everything I thought it would be. Coconut trees, warm weather, not that small of an island, and a very relaxed mission. Yes, indeed, this was an exciting and forever life-changing event. Nevertheless, I soon learned that the assignment was not a critical life-changing moment. Airman First Class (A1C) Anthony "Juice" Jefferis was the assignment.

We met Saturday afternoon, May 25, 1991. I still recall what he was wearing, a black Chicago Bulls hat, short-sleeved white T-shirt, black shorts, and all-white K-Swiss shoes. It took some time for the courtship to begin. I did not care to be in a relationship with anyone. I was unlucky in love, and my mind was made up. I did not come to Guam looking for love. I just wanted to do my 15-month tour and go wherever the Air Force would send me next. Sadly, I embraced being single for the rest of my life, so I just wanted to be left alone. Even though Juice was nice, I was not nice to him. Days after we met, he told me he wanted me to "be his girl," but I said, "No, we can be friends, but nothing more."

Then, one day, on Father's Day 1991, I analyzed A1C Anthony "Juice" Jefferis. He was not a drinker, nor did he smoke. He was not a troublemaker and always treated me kindly. He was also handsome, very outgoing, and funny. After this analysis, I asked myself, "What do I have to lose?" At that moment, I CHANGED my mind. I wanted to find love, and hopefully, I would find it in Anthony. I did not want to be left alone. I wanted to be with someone. I wanted to be with Anthony Jefferis.

About a week passed before I saw him again. This time, I let it be known through my body language, smile, talk, and voice that I was now interested. However, I was not sure he was still interested in me. We had a movie date in his room. His room was complete with the latest audiovisual and stereo equipment and had a nice layout. This was the night of our first kiss. I returned to my room, knowing that I was not alone. November 27, 1993, we were married. Juice got his girl! Moreover, 31 years later, I am still his girl, his good thing!

I share the story of how we met to share some points that we often miss in life:

1. What do YOU have to lose? Imagine if I never took the chance to try again. Relationships require some risk. Based on Anthony's character, he proved to me

he was worth the risk. I was willing to take another courageous leap of faith and try love again.

2. Reminisce and share precious moments in time. Even as I type this chapter, more than a thousand memories of our time in Guam rushed through my mind. I am trying hard to contain my joy over the sweetness of such memories. Sometimes, when the courtship is not so sweet, you and your spouse must remember those moments.

Now that I have shared how we met let me share a few trials we endured in our marriage. In every relationship, there will be trials. I also like to refer to trials as challenges because they affect changes, new perspectives, a new outlook on life, and how to live. We have certainly had our share of challenges.

One of those challenges, which was the scariest, occurred in November 2007 and January 2008. Juice deployed to Iraq in November 2007; I deployed on January 1, 2008. Imagine both spouses deployed to the same country, hours apart, facing extreme danger daily over four to six months. We talked almost every day during our deployments. There were several times Juice had to deploy outside his base perimeter. Whenever he shared with me, he would be on duty off base; immediately, I would go into prayer and fasting mode. The sheer uneasiness of not knowing when my husband would return to base was even more reason for me to pray and fast. I needed to focus on what I trusted God to do instead of focusing on what could happen.

So, imagine the stress placed on him as well. Not only did he have to stay alive and ensure the safety of others, but he also had an even heavier burden on him, worrying about my safety and me. We both knew this situation was beyond our control. Therefore, I did what I knew how to do best–acknowledge that God was in control and surrender to His authority. In addition, He brought us back home safely, minds and bodies intact. Alleluia!

My breast cancer journey was the second most impactful, scariest, yet rewarding challenge. In 2013, the day after Christmas, I was officially diagnosed with DCIS (Ductal Carcinoma In Situ) in both breasts. That was the beginning of a marathon. I clearly remember informing my husband about my cancer diagnosis while he was at work. There was a pause for several seconds before he said, "I have to come home." Every single step of the way, he was always there, always! When I had my initial appointment with each medical team involved, he was in the exam room with me. He was there when I had to decide on the best form of treatment. For the surgeries, throughout the recoveries, and the words of encouragement he gave through it all. He was an indescribably gentle, strong, positive, protective, motivating force, and he still is. Of all the honorable and truthful traits mentioned regarding my husband, I want to elaborate on his gentleness. A main fruit of the Spirit he exercised to perfection during this season. Galatians 5:22-23 (NIV) lists the fruit of the Spirit: "But the fruit of the Spirit is love, joy, peace, forbearance, kindness, goodness, faithfulness, gentleness, self-control. Against such, there is no law."

On January 30, 2014, I had a bilateral mastectomy, the first of four surgeries and the longest procedure lasting about 6.5 hours. The day after this surgery was "THEE" worst part of my cancer journey. Why? The anesthesia had worn off–completely! Now, my chest muscles are responding to the stress from the surgery, hence chest spasms. I also had four very long tubes inserted in both sides of my chest. These tubes helped drain the lymphatic fluid from my chest. A "stripping" process was associated with it that ensured the fluid was cleared from the tubes into a small, plastic container that captured the fluid. Well, it was painful when one of the four tubes was drained. There was a lactic acid-type burning sensation around the insertion site. In addition, that burning, stinging sensation lasted for several seconds. I hated it.

Even though I told the nurses about that specific area, not all of them navigated gently to avoid causing me pain. My husband watched this process as it happened several times throughout the day for about three days. Therefore, he had the process down without ever practicing. When I was released from the hospital, I was not so sure I could drain the tubes myself. However, without question or hesitation, Juice drained my tubes for me. He did this twice a day for two weeks, and he drained them BETTER than any of the nurses did. He always did it gently. He never rushed the process and made sure I was not in pain when he would drain the tube that was most challenging for me.

The war and cancer challenges have positively impacted our marriage in many ways. We already had a healthy, loving marriage. Therefore, these challenges only solidified our marriage.

As a result of the cancer walk, I wrote my first book, *No More Bad Days*. I dedicated a chapter to Juice entitled Superman. There was no way I could write a book without acknowledging him as a critical part of that battle.

Another positive impact the cancer journey specifically had on our marriage is my own perspective of peace. Cancer feeds off many elements. Stress is a major one. I was intentional about desiring to live a stress-free life. Additionally, I was very deliberate about creating a stress-free environment for Juice. The environments I have control over are my home and myself. A peaceful lifestyle is a top priority for me. Therefore, I create a space of peace for Juice and myself in our home. Time carved out for God is extremely, highly critical to that peace. First thing every morning, I dedicate time to prayer, praise, and silence in His presence. Psalm 63:1a instructs us to seek God early. I have learned not only to seek Him early in the morning but early on before making decisions or even having discussions with my husband. I stand by this and have seen the difference it makes in my marriage and the peace it helps maintain in my marriage.

These positive impacts also spill over into what we do to keep our marriage healthy, strong, and fun. One of the things we love to do is go on a nice, long ride on our CanAm Spyder. These are very relaxing moments coupled with intimacy as we touch each other in some way. My hands on his back, him leaning against my chest, his hand on my leg, and us jamming to the sounds piping through the speakers are very intimate moments we enjoy on the Spyder.

Something else we do more is tell one another, "I love you." Especially before one of us leaves the house, it is accompanied by a hug, kiss, and those three powerful little words. We both understand that life is too short. Eight years ago, cancer could have ended my life. During this time, that moment in our marriage was scarier for him than for me.

Another thing we do is address one another by pet names. Rarely do we call one another by our first names. Daddy,

Mommy, Papa, Sun Bear, and Pooka are a few of our favorite pet names for one another.

As I close this chapter, I have some questions for you:

1. What challenge(s) are you facing in your marriage right now?
2. How are you working through the challenge(s)?
3. Are you intentional about creating a space of peace to allow effective communication, healing, and reconciliation?
4. How do you openly communicate what you can do to build and sustain a healthy, fun, romantic marriage?

Chapter 9

Crossing Paths to Brilliant Relationships

By
Contributing Authors
Drs. Dexter and Philomena Marie Johnson

"And do not be conformed to this world [any longer with its superficial values and customs], but be transformed and progressively changed [as you mature spiritually] by the renewing of your mind [focusing on godly values and ethical attitudes], so that you may prove [for yourselves] what the will of God is, that which is good and acceptable and perfect [in His plan and purpose for you]."
Romans 12:2, AMP
#Brilliant
Bible Couple ~ Priscilla and Aquila

W e mostly personify Priscilla and Aquila in the New Testament as a married Christian couple. They were an exemplary Christian Jewish married couple that practiced good relationship ethics, were skilled in their trades as tentmakers and leaders, and were known for their hospitality. The two welcomed the Apostle Paul in their home. The acceptance of Christian Jews was not permissible when Claudius Caesar reigned in Rome (Sharma, 2020). Priscilla and Aquila decided to leave Rome and would later accompany Paul on expeditions to Corinth and Ephesus (Acts 18:1-28, AMP). As we write this chapter, we are on a Mediterranean cruise celebrating our 20th and 21st wedding anniversary and did not know, an opportunity to become authors for this anthology would surface. That has been our love story in a nutshell, and visiting places like Rome and Italy adds to our brilliant saga.

Similarly, as Priscilla and Aquila, we have developed Christian relationship ethics and a love for assisting people of the faith and sharing with unbelievers. Both crossed paths in Corinth with Paul, a tentmaker by trade like the couple, and may have influenced his interest (Caldwell and Ndalamba, 2017, as cited in Sharma, 2020), who is classified as one of the greatest Apostles of all time. For instance, crossing paths and reflecting on our journeys is something we share with couples dating and those married, separated, divorced, and widowed. Sharing our testimonials with audiences has laid the groundwork to help individuals "build relationship intelligence, live life, and inspire and nurture their transformation" (brilliant). Our allegiance to this philosophical thought replicates the great commission when Jesus summons the 11 disciples to a mountain. They were hesitant, as had been the case in their relationship with Christ, through eyewitnesses. He spoke to them concerning the authority given to Him by God in heaven and on Earth. Therefore, Christ admonishes the disciples through His power to go and make disciples globally to instruct, train, and engage the trinity (e.g., the Father, Son, and the Holy Spirit). With baptism as the precursor to living, these engagements, commandments, and understanding of Christ would forever be with them (Matthew 28:16-20, AMP). We endeavor to do the same in assisting couples in understanding their position and Christ.

Another example weaved in scripture was the meeting of Priscilla, Aquila, and Apollos at the Ephesian Synagogue. The three crossed paths at this Synagogue when Apollos had finished delivering his stance on the gospel. Apollos was an Alexandrian and Jew of intellectual eloquence, boldness, and eagerness to share it with the crowd. However, his approach lacked wholeness concerning the workings of Jesus Christ (Sharma, 2020). The couple worked to present their case and bring Apollo's enlightenment, thus becoming his mentors. They used emotional intelligence to enlighten him as mentors by cultivating self-awareness, motivational cues, decision-making, listening, and problem-solving skills. We have practiced fruitful (Galatians 5:22, KJV; Ephesians 5:9, KJV) spiritual intelligence in marriage and working with couples through devotions and prayers. We are reading the Bible as has been done on several occasions. Moreover, to ensure the self-awareness and intelligence to address challenges and enemy attacks. The adversary's patterns are perpetual with infestations to destroy (1 Peter 5:8, ASV) marriages.

Mentors practice extreme care when they guide in non-threatening environments. Nonetheless, Priscilla and Aquila must have formulated a plan to approach Apollos, considering their positional stances and interactions. The two did not interrupt him in the crowd but waited patiently for the right time. Bible scholars emphasized the importance of the wait, such as Hosea when he stated, "Wait on thy God continually" (Hosea 12:6, KJV). Isaiah proclaimed, "And therefore will the LORD wait, that he may be gracious unto you" (Isaiah 30:18, KJV). The Psalmist concluded, "Rest in the LORD, and wait patiently for Him" (Psalm 37:7, KJV)! Christ used storytelling approaches to teach the disciples, believers, and unbelievers on subjects of interest and respond to their inquiries (Matthew 13:34, NCV). He would exercise his brilliance intelligently and at the right time.

We believe God created our love story and have strong convictions on the intersections laid for eventual union Genesis 2:18-25, NKJV; Matthew 19:3-6, NKJV). The love story brings to mind several crossings and mutual attractions that include experiences in early childhood, high school, college, and faith walks. The first known meeting was in early childhood on Gerhardt and Dodge Street off Jefferson Avenue in Buffalo, New York. Moreover, we have different stories regarding the recollection of that meeting. Dexter focused on the recollection of a little girl having six fingers and ponytails that were identifiable, but I thought not because of the removals at birth.

This section shares similar excerpts of unexpected meetings from early childhood to faith encounters in Christ. Those experienced from personal and professional perspectives to honor Christ (Romans 15:1-13, AMP). Furthermore, embedded in the scriptural crossings of

Priscilla and Aquila were Apostle Paul and Apollos. The four had similar evangelistic and ministerial experiences. Their intersections would help to shape them as individuals and to spread the great commission in churches, synagogues, communities, and the marketplace. We endeavor to reach people similarly in their personal and professional relationships, sharing stories for healing and reconciliation (2 Corinthians 5:18, NIV) and building brilliant intelligence.

About Us

Dexter is also known as (aka) "Dr. Dex," the relationship rocket scientist, excellence cultivator, reconciliation ambassador, and aerospace pioneer. I am Philomena, (aka) "Dr. Phil," a higher education advocate, past scholar in residence at Oxford, and career and empowerment strategist. We are co-founders of PhiDex Enterprises LLC, a small woman-owned business designed to help individuals develop excellence in the marketplace. We are certified relationship coaches and have worked in for-profit and nonprofit organizations. Mainly in business, education, and STEM fields and have served in civic organizations, on boards, and possess professional memberships. Together, we are recipients of numerous local, federal, and state awards and proclamations. We have served as family life Pastors, Elders, and Lay Ministers under appointed men and women in leadership. Likewise, we assumed mentorship roles to assist faith constituents, students, and colleagues, and becoming certified foster parents to adopt in Cuyahoga County in Ohio.

We provide four snapshots of crossing paths to share those experiences and perspectives. First, positioning those lenses in early childhood; secondly, high school, thirdly;

college years; and fourth, on the role faith played in their intersections leading to marriage. We know that God created the stepping-stones and paths to enlighten us (Psalm 119:105, KJV) and bridge our relationship with him.

1. Crossing Paths in Early Childhood – We tend to recount when we first crossed paths in our neighborhood in Buffalo, New York. We were born and raised in Buffalo. It was a bustling urban hub with churches and community organizations, schools, libraries, banks, and retail establishments, although often infiltrated by gang presence. We attended Vacation Bible School (VBS) in the summers. Unfortunately, we were not conscious of being in the same parish. Both remember singing the national anthems of VBS, "We are Climbing Jacob's Ladder," and "Jesus Loves Me," having snacks, the classrooms, and activities. We went to Public School #39, which would become Martin Luther King Jr. School. We purchased candies from mom-and-pop stores like the Smith's and Tart's. Avidly, we parked cars in our yards for football and baseball games at the stadium with family and friends. We have flashbacks of Burger Land and Scotties, a Steak House, libraries, and museums. We crossed Lane fields to school, shopped at Loblaws, and went to the laundromat. A bakery factory was a short distance from where sweet smells drifted through the neighborhood. These events remind us of the photographic lens that we are blessed to possess.

2. Crossing Paths in High School – Our vernacular lens of the second crossing in high school revealed that City Honors and Bennett High School had a partnership for gifted students. Dexter went to City Honors, and I went to

Bennett. According to Dexter, his school used space there for extracurricular activities. He and my brother met by playing football and participating in track and field. I was successful at the elementary level in sports and lost interest in high school. We unknowingly did not interact in high school, but he did with my brother.

3. Crossing Paths in Postsecondary Education - The third meeting happened as students of the infamous Trio Programs, the Buffalo Educational Talent Search Programs, and Upward Bound Programs at the State University of New York at Buffalo. Philomena was my math tutor and a student Assistant for Talent Search, and I had become a resident assistant. I was accepted into the school of engineering and Philomena, the school of management, and we are proud graduates of that flagship research institution.

When I first saw Philomena, I thought she was cute and a colleague. My attraction encompassed the smoothness of her skin tone, communication, and wardrobe. Philomena reverberates, admiring my manly features and pecan man skin and having a beard. She liked the idea of me carrying a briefcase and having hairy legs. Moreover, the physical attractions do not surpass our love for Christ (Matthew 22:37, NIV). After that math tutoring session, Philomena and I did not cross paths again at the University. With merged thinking, we still can unfold informal meetings such as my leadership in the gospel choir and her attending concerts—involvement in the same social events and having affiliations with family members and friends. I had worked with some on the campus in student roles.

4. Crossing Paths in Faith – The fourth consists of two pivotal encounters that impacted the development of relational manifestations. The meetings at Greater Faith Bible Tabernacle (GFBT) and Greater Refuge Temple Church (GRTC) in Buffalo, New York. I grew under the tutelage of some great men and women in leadership at both churches, the late Bishop Nathan S. Halton and Apostle Robert L. Sanders, Senior, respectively. My parents were long standing members of GRTC and served in varied capacities. Dexter's parents would share stories about their son, Gregory attending GFBT's Sunday evening services. They would drop him off, and Sanders assisted him back home. His parents and Greg decided to join the GFBT after three decades of faithful membership and service at Memorial Baptist Church. Dexter was a member at Memorial before relocating to Cleveland, Ohio, for a position at NASA, where he is presently an agency-wide Technical Lead for Structural Loads and Dynamics for their Safety Center. Nonetheless, a NASA Fellowship requirement entailed returning to Buffalo, New York, to work at Moog and Veridian, although he had desired to complete it in Switzerland. A senior-level decision had been made due to safety and political concerns.

Dexter and I crossed paths at the GRTC gospel concert and exchanged contact information. A close friend had invited him. After that exchange, we reconnected six years later when he returned to Buffalo for a visit with his parents at GFBT. He confessed that watching me "Praise the Lord" (Romans 15:5, 11, AMP) was an attraction for him. My attraction was based on the same and his walking in the church with a suit and trench coat. After the service, we had communicated wanting to connect for either lunch or dinner. Finally, it was our time and the rest is history. God eventually allowed us the intelligence (John 15:15; Romans 3:22-25, NIV) to connect the dots through our love for Him and the meeting at GFBT. For instance, Dexter's parents sat two rows opposite of me and I never knew they were his parents. Those crossings led to friendship, dating, and marriage in 2001. We share similar experiences of separation and divorce and understanding reconciliation and forgiveness (2 Corinthians 5:18, NIV). However, after volatile divorces, we reclaimed our faith through baptism and comprehended the process of salvation and living a spirit-filled life.

Brilliant Reflection Questions

How do you describe your experiences crossing paths in relationships?
What are your experiences and perspectives on faith and marriage?
How can you connect the dots in your relationships? Use a diagram or SmartArt, for example, to reflect experiences.

Chapter 10

The Ministry of Reconciliation

By
Contributing Authors
Reverends Drs. Joel and Naomi Mitchell

"So from now on we regard no one from a worldly point of view. Though we once regarded Christ in this way, we do so no longer. Therefore, if anyone is in Christ, the new creation has come: The old has gone, the new is here! All this is from God, who reconciled us to himself through Christ and gave us the ministry of reconciliation: that God was reconciling the world to himself in Christ, not counting people's sins against them. And he has committed to us the message of reconciliation. We are therefore Christ's ambassadors, as though God were making his appeal through us. We implore you on Christ's behalf: Be reconciled to God. God made him who had no sin to be sin for us, so that in him we might become the righteousness of God."
2 Corinthians 5: 16-21, NIV
#Reconciliation
Bible Couple ~ Priscilla and Aquila

As we write this chapter, we just celebrated our twentieth wedding anniversary. Anyone married for more than a minute can tell you, it is quite a ride full of many joys, triumphs, and its share of trials and tests. Therefore, you can believe it when we tell you our wedding was a picture-perfect day. We were married on Good Friday and chose the colors red (to symbolize the blood of Jesus) and white. We also had communion to commemorate Christ's broken body and shed blood for us. The day was a celebration, and our community rallied around us to ensure our marriage got off to the best start.

We knew that we had been called together for a purpose. Like Pricilla and Aquila, we have been called to ministry and business as a couple. Therefore, we were serious and excited to fulfill this call with the one person in the world we loved most, next to God.

So later, when we found ourselves at a crossroads in our marriage, we were stunned and disillusioned. Perhaps we thought naïvely that when the enemy crept into our relationship, we would be more prepared, especially since we had committed our lives and marriage to God.

However, we were still ambushed—not because our marriage was not blessed or was incompatible, but because we are human. We found ourselves amid trials, and tests that shattered our confidence in our marriage. We experienced many traumatic events such as emotional infidelity, loss of trust, lack of effective communication, unmet expectations, and illness of a spouse, deferred dreams, and loss of loved ones, unemployment, and unexpected care of an aging/ailing parent. These life-altering events put tremendous pressure on our marriage, and we were not always sure what to do next.

The pain of a rocky marriage is a throbbing, unrelenting pain. Moreover, as humans, we are wired to make that pain go away through our fight-or-flight response system. We begin to ask ourselves; do we stay and fight the stressor or run from it? We often felt like doing both to escape the pain and not deal with it, which led to even more confusion. Instinctively, we wanted to run away.

Finally, the pain became so great that we thought we would be happier apart and that it would be better to start over. It became easier to imagine that the problem was not the situation but one of us. The pain became almost unbearable. The beauty in this pain is that God directed us to His Word and showed us a plan.

We learned that we had lost sight of the roadmap during our hard times. We realized that our vision had become blurred by the vicissitudes of life, and we needed to start again. We needed to return to our source —God. At its core, the ministry of reconciliation is about forgiveness.

Still, we needed to take steps before we were ready to walk in forgiveness. Reconciliation is not simply about forgiving and forgetting; it is about restoration. Our approach to the ministry of reconciliation in marriage came to Naomi as divine inspiration from God. He put this message in her heart several years ago, and we have been walking through this process ever since.

2 Corinthians 5:16-20 gives us the blueprint for lasting reconciliation. Here are some of the major points we have learned:

1. "Therefore, if anyone is in Christ, the new creation has come: The old has gone, the new is here!"
This verse gives us the promise that we can be made new. We do not have to live in the hurt forever. There is a path forward, and it begins with Christ. God tells us that the old is gone. That means we can let go of the pain and rest in the promise that we do not have to suffer under those old hurts. We can be forward-focused instead of living life looking in the rearview mirror and walking in unforgiveness.

2. "All this is from God, who reconciled us to himself through Christ and gave us the ministry of reconciliation."
Naomi likes to say that if God could reconcile the world to Himself, then that means none of our problems are insurmountable. Isn't that powerful? That gives us the confidence to go forward and tackle our issues with the knowledge that we can succeed. It is all possible. We do not have to worry that we will not be able to solve our problems because God has already proven that we will be victorious.

3. ". . . that God was reconciling the world to himself in Christ, not counting people's sins against them."
The most crucial part is "not counting people's sins against them." Of course, we are all human, which means we are predisposed to remember what and who has harmed us. Nevertheless, letting go of old hurts promises us a more fruitful future. Letting go takes practice and may be difficult, but it is not impossible. You may have to seek

counsel to assist you, but you can thrive in learning to forgive. After all, forgiveness is as much for you as it is for your spouse.

Therefore, the first step in reconciliation is to reconcile with God.

That means ensuring that God is the center because that relationship with God is the foundation of everything else we will do. We are of God, meaning if we align with Him and His Word, there is nothing we cannot do. If we have found that we have strayed, we must get back to the source. Our relationship with God is like any other relationship—what we water will grow. We water our relationship with God by going to Him in prayer.

Sometimes, we expect our spouse to fulfill all our needs in a marriage relationship. Isn't that what most marriage vows say? They are supposed to be there for us, for richer or poorer, through hell and high water, sickness, and health. We go into marriage thinking it is going to be the ultimate twosome. However, the truth is that our spouses are only human. If you expect them to be perfect, that will undoubtedly lead to disappointment. We must understand that our spouse is a fallible human being. Because we are married to another human being, we need to look to God to have those voids.

Early in our marriage and ministry, we learned to be still and let God fill those voids. This discipline was not second nature for us, but we had to train ourselves to turn to God. It would be nice if our spouse could always give us the emotional support and validation we seek, but they are limited. Reconciling with God is about getting everything else off the shelf that we may have placed before God. It is coming back to having God as the center. When we return to this relationship with God, all other restorations will flow accordingly.

We can see ourselves through God's eyes when we are in a relationship with God. That perspective, nurture, and freedom cannot come from our spouse; they do not have divine power to liberate us.

The next step is reconciling to self.

Part two of the ministry of reconciliation is reconciling with yourself. After our marriage was broken, we nurtured our relationships with our source—God—and then moved on to the next person who could promote healing in the situation, ourselves.

A popular ritual in modern weddings is the lighting of the unity candle. In this ritual, the bride and groom light their candles using their respective flames to light a singular candle, representing their union. They then blow out their candles and allow the flame from their joint candle to shine.

We find it amazing that right at the beginning, there is symbolism that our individual selves must die for our marriages to thrive, which is untrue. We always tell couples "Don't blow out your candle!" Yes, we must focus on building and strengthening our marital union, but we must maintain our identities. What you bring to the relationship— your identity in Christ, dreams, goals, and visions—matter to the overall health of the marriage.

We got into trouble because we had leaned so far into our marriage that we forgot who we were. As a result, we failed to nourish the singular soul that resided within and allowed ourselves to wither in service of our marriage. We could not figure out what we wanted out of our marriage or lives because we did not know who we were. Likewise, we cannot teach each other how to love or treat us if we do not love ourselves, know ourselves, or even know what we need or want. It takes time and effort to get back to your whole self. The question then becomes, "How does one rediscover themselves?"

We learned that we must get back to the Word. We will always turn to God's Word for clarity and direction. Our quest to bring us back to ourselves led us to Psalm 139:14 (KJV). "I will praise thee; for I am fearfully and wonderfully made: marvellous are thy works; and that my soul knoweth right well."

Read that again: "We are fearfully and wonderfully made." God took His time with us. We are His masterpieces. He looks at us and is proud to see who we are. Joel says, "When God made us, He didn't make junk!" God's works are not just good or "okay." They are marvelous. God is the master craftsman. We must remember that we are both created in God's image, which means we are beautiful and powerful. We learned to remind ourselves that we are one of God's children and worthy of the love we seek; we deserve to have a love that mirrors Christ's love for the church. God's love for us can and will manifest itself in our marriage, but only if we know we are worthy.

We tend to focus on the other person because that is what is comfortable. We often do not stop to think about our role in our marriage problems. However, it is a sign of maturity to say, "This is where I can improve." This self-awareness does not mean that it is our fault if the other person betrayed us. It is about focusing on our behavior because we cannot control anyone else, not letting the stress in our marriage make us hard or bitter. We had to practice not letting our problems with one another suck all the joy out of our life. We had to begin shedding the weight of the past and become more future-focused.

This approach requires that we look inward and deal with whatever is weighing us down, whether it is low self-esteem, immaturity, selfishness, control issues, or worse. However, of course, we did not come to this marriage as perfect people. Therefore, work can still be done on our end, even if it is warming our hearts up to the idea of forgiveness.

After we reconciled with God and submitted to the personal work on ourselves, we reconciled to one another by picking up the pieces of our broken marriage, reframing the vision of what we thought our marriage should have been, and moving forward by the leading of the Holy Spirit. In her book, "The Power of a Praying Wife," Stormie O'Martian states that one of her prayers around her marriage is, "Lord, I want my husband to have a new wife, but let it be me." Sometimes, it is easier to get divorced and seek a different person. However, we like this sentiment from Stormie O'Martian. Likewise, Joel says, "I want my wife to have a new husband, but Lord, let it be me." Each of us can make a change to better the whole.

Questions

How is your alignment with God?
How do you see yourself inside your marriage?
Does your marriage appear beyond repair?

Chapter 11

Love: Friendship Set on Fire

By

Contributing Authors William and Larrissa Parker

"Love is patient, love is kind. It does not envy, it does not boast, it is not proud. It does not dishonor others, it is not self-seeking, it is not easily angered, it keeps no record of wrongs. Love does not delight in evil but rejoices with the truth. It always protects, always trust, always hopes, always perseveres. Love never fails."
1 Corinthians, 13: 4-8, NIV
#Love&Restoration
Bible Couple ~ David and Abigail

W hen we think of couples in the Bible that we can relate to, it would have to be David and Abigail.

Although their story is short, there are so many similarities and unique parallelisms that we connect with as a couple. William, like David, the youngest sibling in his family, and Larrissa, attractive and wise, like Abigail, is known as the peacemaker. David and Abigail's story is one of second chances, the pursuit of reconciliation, and God's intervention. A story of a future King and a woman of great intellect and beauty who developed a friendship set on fire. Despite their dramatic beginnings, flaws, and imperfections, their destiny collided to form an unexpected union of matrimony.

We met in England 21 years ago while serving in active duty Air Force. We were two single parents with custody of our children, rediscovering ourselves while learning to love again. We encountered each other in this foreign land with caution, as this was our first relationship after experiencing divorce. Despite our reservation to protect our hearts from the pain of failed relationships, we allowed nature to take its course and embraced our evolving friendship. We let our guards down and opened the possibility to love again. The friendship eventually caught fire; as they say, the rest is history. In this case, there is *His* story and *Her* story. Walk with us down memory lane as we recant the individual viewpoints of our encounter.

His Story

As I penned this story concerning David, I could not help but wonder what his first impression was of such a beautiful woman he would later know as Abigail. The first sight of Larrissa had me witness firsthand God's angel here on earth.

Maybe that is an exaggeration of my first impression, but not much. I walked behind her table to play my favorite arcade game, Galaxy but was quickly distracted by this very attractive young lady. I immediately noticed her beauty and radiant smile as she sat amongst a group of children at a Pizza Parlor table. She was so intently engaged with the children that she never even noticed me. As a single parent with custody of my son Brenden (6) and daughter Bria (4), this was the first time I ever considered a young lady in my life other than my daughter.

By this time, I had learned to forgive those in my past. I learned how to become whole after feeling like life had been broken into pieces. I found peace and was content as a single parent, loving my children's resilience after divorce. Therefore, with this wholeness and awareness of self, I paused the video game I was playing and leaned across a small partition dividing us to ask her a question. Confident but somewhat nervous at the same time, I said, "Hello, are all of these your children?" I immediately thought, "Wow, why would you ask her that." It was then I realized how weak my game was.

After all, I had not had to do this in over a decade. It was too late to recant, so I patiently waited for her response. After what felt like a lifetime, she eventually replied. Captivated by her beauty and warm countenance, I did not comprehend her words. She appeared a little tired, and I thought this was not the best opportunity for a conversation. I did not even ask her to repeat her response. I just nodded with a smile and slowly turned back to finish my arcade game. By this time, my son was done stuffing himself with pizza and came back to join me. Although that was the end of our conversation, her radiant smile and Louisiana accent were etched in my heart and mind. I hoped to see her again sooner than later, but the sooner never came. It would be months before our paths crossed again.

Her Story

Yes, we indeed met in a Pizza Parlor in England. After work, I volunteered to watch a few of my co-workers' children while they bowled in the Medical Group's bowling league. Although I was exhausted, I fulfilled my commitment to watching these five high-spirited children. To pass the time, I took the children to grab a bite to eat at a nearby Pizza Parlor. Thank goodness, the parlor was scantly occupied, and I could locate a space for the children and me near the gaming area. This space was perfect. It provided entertainment for the children and became a place of refuge for me. I was still in my uniform, beyond tired and not feeling or looking my best.

As I was downloading mentally, a handsome gentleman leaned across the partition to ask me, "Are these your children?" I would admit it took a moment for me to respond. Although one child was mine, I thought the question was laughable as children of various races surrounded me and all close in age. Nevertheless, I smiled because I acknowledged it was William's way of engaging in small talk with me. I politely answered, "No, just babysitting for a few of my co-workers." While this was the extent of our conversation, I could not help but notice how handsome, well put together and confident he was. He was dressed well, and I could sense he had a great sense of style. I desired to engage more with William but could not muster the energy to do so. Fortunately, the opportunity was not lost, as I would see him over the next few months, secretly admiring him from afar. I often wondered if he even noticed or remembered me. Nevertheless, as a single parent to a four-year-old son, Vontez Jr., affectionately known as T.J., dating was not my priority at the time.

Our First Date

As fate would have it, we had another one-on-one encounter months later. I responded to an advertisement via phone, and low and behold, the guy who answered was, yes, you guessed it, the guy from the pizza parlor, William. Although we never exchanged names during our initial encounter, I recognized his voice immediately. During this call, he wasted no time seizing the moment and asking me out on a lunch date. I was excited because this was music to my ears; although I wanted to remain composed, an instantaneous "yes" flowed through my smile.

Over our lunch date, I became even more intrigued with William. His intellect captivated me, which caused me to give him my undivided attention willingly. For a brief moment, it was as if we were the only two patrons in the restaurant. Nothing and no one seemed to matter, as I was utterly fixated on every word that proceeded from his mouth. However, this blissful moment came and went within minutes after William told me that he would be relocating to the states within the next three months. Upon hearing this news, I was disappointed, so to disguise my disappointment, I stated, "That's okay, and I'm not looking for anything serious." To my surprise, William said, "Likewise." Despite these declarations, we spent every day after our initial lunch meeting enjoying each other's company. We spent an enormous amount of time together talking and hanging out after work. We even traveled throughout Europe, making lasting memories while being intently aware of our short timeline. William and I discussed everything and challenged each other with the most thought-provoking conversations. He kept me smiling. Through our time together, I learned about William's character. He was a Godly man, a courageous leader, and one who cherished family. He quickly became my best friend; I was truly falling in love with this man. As William would say, "Love is friendship set on fire." Yes, I am now thinking my King has arrived.

When good things come to an end (Larrissa)

Finally, it was time for William to relocate to Maryland while I stayed behind to complete my tour of duty in Europe. I had never encountered a man like William, a Man of God and one with so much drive. Not only was he everything I wanted in a mate, but he was also everything I knew I deserved. As David did for Abigail, William created a safe place for me, allowing me to love him without limits. We agreed to continue our relationship long distance. We spoke often and even visited each other every three to four months. We acquired expensive phone bills during this relationship phase and accumulated frequent flyer miles. Although we started our long-distance relationship confidently, believing it would be a breeze, after two years, the inevitable occurred. The long-distance carried a weight too great to sustain, so we ended the relationship. I have to admit I was devastated, and it took some time for me to move on; however, I had to accept that this good thing had come to an end.

Breaking away and coming back together

As the saying goes, "there is sunshine after the rain." Five years and several failed relationships later, William and I reconnected. As I write this, I am reminded of the lyrics to the song, "Reunited and it feels so good." I was elated to have William back in my life. During our time apart, we had little contact with each other. Therefore, as one could imagine, we had much catching up to do. From my perspective, fate brought us back together. William had become the standard, which no one managed to measure up to. Reconnecting with him gave me life, and I could exhale and love again. However, once again, we found ourselves in a long-distance relationship. I was now in North Dakota, and William was in Hawaii. After dating for approximately five months, I came to a crossroads in my military career and decided to separate from active duty. At the same time, William completed his tour in Hawaii and was relocating back to Maryland. I decided to follow William to Maryland in hopes of continuing what we'd started, and this time, I was hoping we would have our happily ever after.

The life of our blended family

Well, it is my turn to speak. I will pick it up from here. Larissa, like Abigail, was wise and knew how to get what she wanted. I may add a woman of many words as well, of course in esteem. Therefore, after two years of dating, I proposed, she accepted, we married and became one.

Mark 10:8 (NIV) reads, "…and the two will become one flesh. So, they are no longer two but one flesh"

Now with all our children combined, Bria and T.J. (14), Brenden (16), and Bryan (24), life as we once knew it had changed. We were all excited about beginning our new life together, but we did not anticipate the unique challenges, which manifested soon after. We faced new challenges as we began life together as a family. These challenges included clashing different parenting styles, learning to live interdependent of each other versus independently, and readjusting after children returned from summer breaks with respective parents. The smooth rhythmic flow we had while dating was no longer. IT JUST GOT REAL! We were so enamored and blinded by our new union that we did not cultivate a proper foundation for our children. At times, we still operated as two single families under one roof.

We did not even fully consider what our children thought of our decision to marry. Therefore, merging families was not as seamless as we thought. We were saved but felt out of alignment with God. We were doing life according to our plans and not God's plan. Therefore, with our reliance on self and not God, we struggled. At times, it felt as if our marriage was on life support, and we could not see our future. Many times, we were not even certain that we would be able to hold on to our marriage. We even found ourselves on the brink of calling it quits. Have you ever been in a place in your relationship where it just became too overwhelming? We were at this point and were depleted of energy to carry on, BUT GOD.

Restoration

"Do not be anxious about anything, but in every situation, by prayer and petition, with thanksgiving, present your requests to God…" (Philippians 4:6, NIV).

We were in a place of despair and desperately in need of restoration. We were at a breaking point, in which we surrendered our family to God. It was then God intervened and breathed new life into our marriage. He became the center of our marriage. He answered our spoken requests and fulfilled our desire to live in peace and harmony. We were determined to MAKE MARRIAGE GREAT. I, Like David, had to stand up to become king and headship of my household. My wife established herself as a helpmate and, like Abigail, was a true peacemaker. "Who can find a virtuous woman? For her price is far above rubies" (Proverbs 31:10, KJV). "I found her!" My wife became my best friend, prayer partner, and confidant through our journey. We aligned with God and forfeited missing out on our blessings and, ultimately, our destiny. We allowed God to order our footsteps toward righteousness and become more intentional with our obedience toward God. He had given us this ministry of marriage and extended his grace and mercy towards our family. For that, we are forever grateful. When you feel that there is no blueprint for marriage, open the Bible, it is the living word of God, the breath of life, and the word of God will change the trajectory of your situation for the better. We are living examples.

Marriage is good work, and you must choose to love each other daily. Keep loving. Keep growing and keep God first. We sincerely hope our story of *love* and *restoration* gives you the fortitude never to give up, to trust in God, and allow Him to order your steps.

"Brothers and sisters, as I said, I know I have not arrived, but there's one thing I am doing: I'm leaving my old life behind, putting everything on the line for this mission" (Philippians 3:13, VOICE).

We are not perfect, but God can give you perfect peace as you strive to Make Marriage Great!

We want to share some secret ingredients to our marriage:

1 Cup of faith

Dash of friendship

Pinch of resilience

1 Tablespoon of patience

Sprinkle of love

Teaspoon respect and appreciation for one another

Directions: Start with your friendship and add a pinch of resilience and faith. (May get lumpy but keep stirring). Blend in a tablespoon of patience (please do not skip this part) and garnish with respect and appreciation (this is a must-have, no substitutions). Now sprinkle with Love and serve daily.

Question

What are you trusting God to do for your marriage?

Chapter 12

Keep The Enemy Out

By
Contributing Authors Rodney and Michele Peake

"Love is patient, love is kind. It does not envy, it does not boast, it is not proud. It does not dishonor others, it is not self-seeking, it is not easily angered, it keeps no record of wrongs. Love does not delight in evil but rejoices with the truth."
1 Corinthians 13:4-6, NIV
#Love
Bible Couple ~ Adam and Eve

A great marriage is not a problem free marriage. A great marriage is a marriage that can rebound, be restored, or renovated when necessary. A great marriage honors and pursues God's intended design for marriage. Adam and Eve let the enemy creep in, and as a result, they were separated from God. We also let the enemy creep in, and as a result, we were separated from one another.

How did the enemy get in our marriage in the first place? Well, with Adam and Eve, they both did what God asked them NOT to do, and in their case, they ate the fruit from the tree of the knowledge of good and evil. So, what had we allowed the enemy to make us do and not do?

Sitting down to write our chapter, we had to take a hard look at our marriage to answer the question, "How did we let the enemy in during times of trouble? How were we able to kick him back out?"

Her - Like Eve

We were married pretty young, at 25 and 26. The first several years of our marriage were great. We even made it past that seven-year itch everyone warned us about. We truly enjoyed our early years of marriage, despite having several miscarriages. I suspect Adam and Eve also enjoyed their paradise in the beginning.

So, what happened? Why was I feeling invisible in my own house again as I did when my husband was grieving the loss of his mom several years prior? I often wondered why Eve was out there talking to a snake and where was Adam at the time? Was he not spending enough time with her? Is that how she befriended an enemy?

One day, it was as if someone picked up my entire house and shook it until everyone fell out, the children, us, and even the dog! I felt so emotionally wounded. After two decades of marriage, my heart had been broken. I had never known that feeling before and was no longer valued by the man who promised always to love and cherish me. I had just finished teaching a Bible study lesson where lives were being impacted. We were counseling other couples, and still, our home was under such severe attack, especially our marriage.

Like with Adam and Eve, the enemy is still trying to use our weaknesses and fears against us today. I was no exception to his schemes, and truth be told, our biggest enemy is ourselves.

I remember I had just returned from Africa, and my oldest took off to another state unannounced. My youngest was using marijuana against our wishes. After my husband's two strokes and cancer diagnosis, it felt like the furnace was being turned up like never before. The negativity in my house and marriage began to magnify. I grew increasingly tired of the arguing, blaming, and what seemed like an almost complete shutdown from my husband - emotionally, spiritually, and physically.

I Let The Enemy In

So, what was my contribution to what was happening? As a woman of God, did I let the enemy in? As I pondered this question with God, I realized I had inwardly given up. I, too, shut down. I closed the door to my heart as a self-preservation mechanism. Once I closed the door to my heart, the enemy gained even more ground.

As a result, I stopped praying for us. I, like Eve, was beginning to believe the enemy's lies based on what I saw and felt. My flesh was taking over for sure. I began to think my husband would not change and that the marriage God designed would not come to pass. That I was not valuable because he no longer made me feel valuable. I began to trade in my time with God as I once had with negative thoughts. I stopped seeing my value through God's eyes and started looking to my husband for that value, and boy, what a trap of the enemy that was.

After finding inappropriate text messages and my husband's comments on social media pages, I completely gave up, and we were separated right in our house. It felt like the enemy had won. I got a full-time job and began to save money to move out.

The Turning

But God has a way. One day, in my devotion time with Him, I cried out and asked for His healing over my wounded and broken heart. God said you have to start over. In my mind, I thought about Joseph, who had a do-over, the woman with the issue of blood who got a new start, and everyone knows Job and his wife had a renovation. I felt deep down inside this could not be restored. Rod and I needed much renovation.

As a wife, a mother, and a woman of God, it was critical for me to still follow God in all my heartache and pain because I did not have another place to put it. It had to be God. I could still feel His Love and His presence. It was an opportunity for me to apply scripture again and cast all my cares upon Him who cares for us.

Some of the things God compelled me to look at were my own unforgiveness and letting go of the past. I thought I had forgiven everything, but God showed me there was still more in my way blocking me from the marriage I desired to have. Once I asked God to reveal and help me forgive, I could start to see with a fresh set of eyes again.

I also had to pray for us and have a tangible battle plan where God was at the center. This was critical since my heart was closed, and it would take only God to open it back up again.

I sought Christian counseling for strength, guidance, and encouragement, and God sent the right individuals. This was important because I was used to always pouring out, and God instructed me to get counseling for myself. Things started to turn around, and I could see the possibilities again.

Him - Like Adam

As I reflect on the past 29 years, there were times of extreme happiness and times of disappointment and unhappiness. When I think about it, I can see how the enemy successfully infiltrated our relationship and my role in allowing him that space!

The first memory was how I handled the death of my mother. The day my mom passed, my world was flipped upside down. Being spiritually immature, I did not know how to lean on Christ.

Internalizing

As an only child whose father left him, I learned to internalize things during difficult times, and this time was no different, or so I thought. This time, I had a wife and two daughters. The pain was so unbearable I saw no other way than to internalize it more profoundly than ever before. In hindsight, there was no seeking Christ, no praying, and no asking for prayer, no making myself available to anyone but this new pain and myself. Little did I know by internalizing my pain and blocking everyone out, I would isolate my wife and kids. I had left my wife to tend to everything as I checked out to deal with my pain. I did not allow my wife to talk to me, cry, or love me. Now I know that I never helped her deal with the pain of our loss by isolating her. She lost a mother-in-law, after all. I had allowed the enemy to creep his ugly head in by isolating her. In turn, he was able to plant doubt in her mind about my love for her. What a big mistake.

I let the enemy creep in by holding on to unforgiveness. I held onto past hurt, pain, and anger from my mother's sickness. I used it to blame my wife. Adam also blamed his wife, Eve, for his sin.

The Incident

I began to magnify things in my mind after Pauline passed on. One incident that I held onto for years was during her last days. I was supposed to be at her bedside doctor's visit. It was usually my responsibility to drop my daughter off at school. However, because of the forecast, I asked my wife to drop my daughter off. The storm caused traffic jams. When my mother asked the doctors if she was dying, they told her yes. There is nothing we can do. When I got to the hospital 15 minutes late, she relayed the message with tears in her eyes. I was mortified! I carried that moment in my heart with anger for years—at both the doctors and my wife.

I became unloving toward my wife for many years after. This allowed the enemy to gain an even bigger foothold in my marriage. I now realize my struggle with holding onto offenses and my abandonment issues brought on internalizing things from my father leaving. I thought it was better to keep my issues and thoughts to myself. It seemed safer because I would not have to worry about someone leaving me again like my father left me to no fault of my own.

The Turning

The turning point that showed me that I needed to change was when God showed me that I was losing my gift (My Wife). I was losing her by not caring for her emotionally, physically, or spiritually. He showed me that I was not displaying love and not allowing love to cover a multitude of sins.

My anger was festering. I internalized my troubles and disappointments, causing countless unnecessary arguments, pain, and suffering. Being broken-hearted by my mother's passing all significantly impacted my hypertension, and eventually, I had a major stroke. I had let the enemy use my mind to turn my body into a weapon against me. Nevertheless, I thank God that He knew, and He healed me!

Love covers a multitude of sins. Today, a stronger prayer life, meditating, and reading God's Word are helping me to display a better 1 Corinthians 13 kind of love towards my wife. I have learned that it is essential to communicate your feelings, desires, and sometimes disappointments, but in love. I had to allow my heavenly father to teach me how to be a better husband, to forgive, and heal through his Word and wise counsel.

1. We want to challenge couples to keep Christ as the third chord in their marriage, whether struggling or not. This is the key to kicking and keeping the enemy out! Allow Jesus Christ to be the deciding factor in all your marital matters. The survival of your marriage depends on it. Then, pursue the 1 Corinthians 13 love. True love is not rude, is not self-seeking, is not easily angered, and it keeps no record of wrongs. Also, both of you must walk in God's grace and forgiveness towards one another.

2. We are allowing God to renovate us individually so that we will be stronger and better together collectively. When you think of a renovation, some old stuff has to go, and some new stuff has to be added. We are still on this journey of becoming stronger as one, and prayerfully God will use our marriage and yours to show the world that GOD can heal a broken heart, soften a hard heart and change the path or direction of any marriage.

5 Peake bonus Points to Ponder
1. Date again and try new places!
2. Pray TOGETHER!
3. Give your spouse their Love Language often!
4. Re-start, if necessary!

5. Execute a vision/direction for your marriage, and write it down!

Questions

Does your marriage reflect a 1 Corinthians 13 love?

Have you let the enemy creep into your marriage?

Chapter 13

From the Bedroom to the Boardroom Balancing Marriage, Business & Ministry as MarriageCEOs

By
Contributing Authors
Drs. Dwight and Deidra Roussaw

"Come with me by yourselves to a quiet place and get some rest."
Mark 6:31, NIV
#Gratitude
Bible Couple ~ Priscilla and Aquila

I n a marriage, both spouses should be intentional about becoming teammates! To become effective teammates, establish an authentic friendship that is unmovable and unshakable.

We met in grammar school. Deidra said Dwight had a crush on her, yet Dwight said Deidra had a crush on him. Deidra was not allowed to have a boyfriend, so we were only friends. The two of us reconnected years later, dated eight years, and married on August 8, 1998.

We worked together in business and ministry in many capacities. In 1999, we started a business together in the travel industry. In 2009, we started a marriage ministry (TWOgetherMarriages). In 2010, Deidra started a wives' ministry (TrulyWed Wives); in 2011, Dwight began a husbands' ministry (Husbands United). Therefore, we have been working together for a couple of decades. Our mission is to teach couples how to balance business and ministry because sometimes, working with your spouse is difficult. We call this making it work, from the boardroom to the bedroom.

In a marriage, both spouses should be intentional about becoming teammates. To become effective teammates, establish an authentic friendship. The friendship should be unmovable and unshakable. As husband and wife, one of the implications of their vows is that they will be supporting the growth of each other. When they became a couple, they began to work together, rather than independently. The word of God says, "The two shall become one."

We need some aspects in our life to help us bring balance and understanding of whatever challenges we have when we go through storms because we are going to go through storms. I remember one of our pastors said, either you are in a storm, coming out of a storm, or you are getting ready to go into a storm.

We should have an open mind and humble ourselves. When facing challenges in the marriage, we encourage husbands to remember why they asked their wives to meet them at the altar and wives to remember why they agreed to meet their husbands at the altar.

If one spouse wants a break, we should be breaking together from work. We should not take a break from the marriage but take a break from the day-to-day operations. A few times a year, spouses should attend an outing to enhance the marriage. This could be a summit, conference, or retreat. They should be enhancing their marriage at least one or two times a year. We take a vacation as a couple every year, our Marriage on Fire Retreat, and a vacation with our family, the Families on Fire Getaway.

Priscilla and Aquila from Acts 18 were a couple who had a business and were preaching the gospel. They worked well together.

If you want to balance your business, marriage, and your home, you must be able to have the same mindset. The skill set is not necessarily to work in the same place or even have the same profession. Yet, understanding what the demands are for one another's occupation to do what you need to do and not come up with shortcomings. Sometimes we do certain things, which we do not consult with our spouse. Therefore, we should be consulting with our spouses on certain things. When we talk about Priscilla and Aquila, we can see how our lives have been transformed into a couple similar to Priscilla and Aquila. They worked alongside one another in ministry.

When Priscilla and Aquila were mentioned in the scriptures, they were always together but still were serious about their faith in the Lord and ministry. Their goal was to please the Lord by ministering to others about the love of Christ. They were lovers and friends and were inseparable. The Bible says the church is a province of Asia sending you greetings. Priscilla and Aquila, greet you warmly. In the Lord, and so does the church that meets in their house. When we started our marriage ministry, we did not know that our story was very similar to Priscilla and Aquila, but it is such a blessing.

In 2008, we hit a roadblock in our marriage while preparing and planning Retie the Knot (renewing our vows) at Sandals Resort in Negril, Jamaica. The Lord revealed that my husband was having an emotional affair and did not even know he was involved. He was a certified Christian counselor, he was counseling a single woman with various issues, and she started liking him. Deidra was resistant because, at that time, she felt that was the icing on the cake. She was done with the marriage.

We were going through in our marriage! Deidra wanted to leave the marriage because things were not how she thought they should have been. God gave her permission to leave, so she hired a moving company. She took some of the furniture while leaving some of the furniture in the house for Dwight. Yet, the day the movers came, Dwight saw that Deidra was serious, and he started packing. Deidra asked him, "Where are you going?" He said, "We're moving." Deidra was shocked and against it. Dwight said to her, "I'm covering you, and God put me here to cover you!"

However, Deidra thought about their friendship and the business. They started the business in 1999, and she realized she did not create a strategy to separate or revise the business. Therefore, with that being said, our business helped save our marriage because we had to travel with one another. Since we were both certified Christian counselors, Dwight did not want to do counseling, yet he wanted the marriage.

Without us realizing it, the Lord gave us a strategy to bring healing to our marriage. Although I, Deidra, became a bitter wife for over a year, the marriage was healed in three parts. First, we had to travel to Sandals "Couples Only" Resort in Ocho Rios, Jamaica, for business. Since Sandals is a lovely romantic resort, it is impossible to be at Sandals Resort and not enjoy the romance that is always in the air. The second thing that happened is that we took a course for our marriage. Deidra found a marriage ministry course for marriage leaders. Although we were not leading a marriage ministry or group at that time, we had been in leadership since 2004, so our application was accepted. We were not taking the course for ministry but our marriage. The marriage course helped us because we both could authentically purge individually and collectively. This is now a course that we currently teach to couples. It is called Dynamic Marriage. The third thing happened when we both had to travel to Beaches Resort in Turks and Caicos. While we were traveling to Beaches in Turks and Caicos, the Lord showed up in a mighty way. The resort manager put us in their new Villa's best room, which was so romantic. The Lord spoke to Deidra while she was outside leaning on a pine tree, crying out to him, and as he talked to her, at the same time, he spoke to Dwight. God told us to leave our issues on the island.

Furthermore, we needed to unite as a couple and get into a position for our healing. We left our issues on the island, and that is how our marriage was healed. This is how our business played a significant part in saving our marriage.

That next year we started a ministry. There were not many outreach marriage ministries, so we were unclear about how to navigate, but God gave us the vision systematically. TrulyWed Wives was birthed because wives needed the wives' tribe, and the Lord showed Deidra how to use her creative vision that he gave her as a gift, which also led to the Wives on Fire Dialogue. Dwight launched Husband United after the husbands saw their wives growing, and the Husbands Huddle was birthed.

Another thing that happened that year, in August of 2008, we Retied the Knot in Jamaica. Our Bishop and Pastor went with us because they knew that we were struggling in our marriage, and they were a part of our support system. We had over 20 people who traveled with us.

On our trip, as a sendoff celebration, our Bishop paid for us to get on a Jet Ski. This occurred when our ceremony was over and before the reception began. Since during that time, Dwight and I were not on one accord, Dwight was leaning to the right, and Deidra was leaning to the left on the Jet Ski. The Jet Ski toppled over into 35 feet of water.

We both almost drowned! Once we went underwater, the rescue boat had to come to rescue us. Neither of us had life preservers, Deidra had on her wedding gown, Dwight had on his suit. All their family and friends were on the shoreline watching and were fearful of us drowning.

While we were underwater, the Lord was speaking to us. However, neither one of us knew this until a year later because Deidra returned home bitter, and Dwight was full of pride. Our communication was off for nearly an entire year before our marriage was totally restored.

During the time under the water, the Lord said to Deidra, "He could take me out right now, but he had ministry for me to do." Astonishingly, He said the same thing to Dwight. Today, because the life rescue team had to go rescue us both, Dwight loves to claim, "We were baptized together!"

A takeaway from their Island vow renewal mishap is that our Bishop said to us, "It's you two against the world." Today, this is the way we view and operate our marriage. Now, both of us are marriage coaches and marriage mentors, where Dwight coaches and mentors husbands and Deidra coaches and mentors wives. We are in marriage together, in business together, and in ministry together. We call this MBM, Marriage, Business, and Ministry. We give couples strategies and techniques using tools to work together and take your marriage from the bedroom to the boardroom as MarriageCEOs.

It is imperative to ensure that you are both doing what you are supposed to do when you are supposed to. It is not easy to balance your marriage at times, but both spouses can help bring the overall balance into the marriage. It is not either or, it is and, and both. As we said earlier, Dwight and Deidra have been in business since 1999 and ministry since 2009. It has not always been easy, but we were determined to have a balanced lifestyle as a married couple in the marketplace.

Praying together is our ultimate strategy. Prayer is an essential component. When we pray, we are talking to God as a unit. We must learn how to pray together about the situation, whether in the bedroom or the boardroom. It could be our marriage, it could be our business, it could be our ministry, but we must pray. Couples should have a couples' devotion weekly at the least. We have couples' devotion on Saturday mornings. We also have a date night once a week on Friday evening. We have a lot of fun when we go out on date night. We ought to be inspiring, uplifting, and encouraging one another. We should constantly affirm one another. We must be that spiritual pillar of support for one another.

In conclusion, both spouses bring their unique personalities into the marriage, which is not always bad. Dwight came from a very mellow background, while Deidra went from a very structured background. They both wanted the atmosphere opposite of what they had during their upbringing. Dwight desired structure while Deidra yearned for mellow. After their 10th year of marriage, they both learned that they could have both, which provided astounding balance. Watching other couples' devotion to one another was key in guiding us. Praying and reading the Bible together is a game changer for our date nights and us. Forgiveness allows us to continue to grow in grace and knowledge. Learning forgiveness allowed us to write a book titled *The Forgiveness Project (The Art of Forgiving)*, which will launch at their 11th Marriage on Fire Retreat.

Question

What strategies can you create to affair-proof your marriage?

Chapter 14

Becoming The New ME To Become A Better WE

By
Contributing Authors Fulton and Cortne' Lee Smith

*"My flesh and my heart may fail,
but God is the strength of my heart
and my portion forever."*
Psalm 73:26, NIV
#NEW
Bible Couple ~ Abigail and Nabal to Abigail and David

Becoming the new me to become a better we is our desire. If you did not know, we married within 45 days of meeting each other. We knew that we had the experience of marriage, what it looked like, and the work and effort it took to be married.

However, we did not bring the same people into the relationship from a previous marriage. We did not bring who we were as a wife or a husband to another person. Those relationships had reached death. Furthermore, if you do not know, no two people are alike. So we are going to take you on this journey and behind the scenes with us how you really should be building to become a new me to become a better we. Every day, we should be becoming a better version of ourselves so that we can become a better help in our relationships to keep us together. Otherwise, what will happen is that the old version will cause death in our new relationship because we are not evolving, growing, and staying connected. So stay along for this growth journey so your relationship can grow to be the best version of itself.

Moving Into Each Other's Space

It all began on the 46th day; I DO day. We got married on New Year's Eve 2012. Therefore, at the beginning of the New Year in 2013, we declared it was going to be a bright new year for us. However, we still had two separate households. At this point, we had to learn how to combine our families. We began to move out of one place and into another place that belonged to someone else. So how do you move into someone else's space that their previous spouse already set up without offending them or dishonoring the memory beyond the painting by moving and readjusting and allocating space for a new person(s)? Please know the best version of ourselves did not happen overnight. This is not an overnight process in your relationships. I want you to understand that you are always going to be moving into each other's space.

As you move into each other's space mentally, physically, or emotionally when navigating this new space, you must recognize that you must be flexible with what is already there. You have to be already open to adjusting yourself to become something new in this space. The new space requires you to become a new vessel. How do you become a new vessel? You have to identify your new role and what is needed in this space. I am not talking about just the paint on the walls. I am talking about in this place. What does your spouse require of you in this new space? It requires you to connect to find out what each other needs in this new space. The new space is the first step in identifying the transition from one person to another. The second step is how this process begins as you enter this new space, which is a daily space, their emotional space changes based on how they are affected by internal and external issues. Our external space weighed heavy on our relationship with my spouse and me. We were both on the road. We were both working. Our space was dramatically affected because he was on the road driving while I spent 80% of my work time in hotels. The on-the-road training and the outside constantly affected our mental, emotional, and physical space, and we had to learn how to navigate these new spaces daily. Please take into account people's new space every day because of the outside influences and inside influences that are going on.

Whether it is the kids, school, the job, or all those things, examine your space, adjust, and navigate what type of vessel you need to be that day. You might need to be a welcoming vessel by allowing the person to pour into you, vent, or just receive and not give nothing in return. You may need to be a plate and serve up everything or a fork and do all the work and the heavy lifting. When recognizing the space, ensure that the atmosphere stays in a place of nurturing and peace. As you learn to navigate spaces, be aware of spaces with volatile arguments or outbursts and death-defying silence. This is a dangerous space, and you need to avoid being in this place. Do not be afraid of new spaces of peace. Take residence in the new space called peace and learn how to daily maintain this peace. Take the time to become a new you to recognize who you need to be for the betterment of everything that will work for the good of your relationship.

Nurture to Multiply

Next, after we move from the new space, we have to recognize where we are going to go after this space. We got a mental, physical and emotional adjustment in this new space. We must learn to work together in this space because we want to grow. We do not want to have what we used to have. We want to be able to multiply what we have. Every day we should multiply by adding seeds to each other and watering each other's interests. How do you say we do that? We have to take the time to find out what helps each other grow. We have to be nurturers. We have to be nurturers because I know it is very common to say that the woman is the nurturer, but it is we. Therefore, in this conversation, as we become nurturers, we have to identify what it is in that area(s) to invest time, energy, and resources into the other. What is the seed that is already planted within that person?

First, some things in our spouse will need to be uprooted so the new will not be choked by predetermined growth from the past. We do not need to nurture bad habits from the past, nor do we need to leave weeds in our new space. That is why I say yes. Sometimes it is great to have a past reference in a relationship, but for us, I had 20 years, and he had 32 years. There are several past relationships that we had and baggage that became weeds. It was good for them, but it is not good for us now. As I had shared, we had a lot of manure going on in our relationship that was not helping to nurture what we needed right now. It was just creating a lot of funkiness. Therefore, in this place, we had to realize what was not working.

As we began to nurture each other, we identified the seeds of the good things in each other. We began to appreciate and give praise for those things each day instead of focusing on the things that were not necessarily the best. This is an opportunity as a nurturer to see and seek out the best in our spouse; you know, everybody talks about the potential. I am not talking about the potential of a person because we cannot make somebody be who he or she are not. Nevertheless, I am talking about what you already see them working with what you see them doing. How can you multiply that? How can you nurture those seeds? What is it that you can do? Can you give them the time, space, and advice or put them around the people and create those circles for them to become a better version of themselves so you can become a better we? Do you allow them the space to navigate for themselves so that they can find that place? That sunny place or that shady place that they need to be in so that they can grow to their best version of themselves. How you nurture your spouse in this relationship is key to how you multiply in your relationship. If all you are throwing dirt on them daily, constantly piling it on, there is no way, no matter how much they try to break through. They will never grow unnurtured. Make sure you are not putting on more weight than they can bear in the relationship. Make sure that you are taking the opportunity to take out some of the weeds, pouring back the water, and you are doing the gardening that needs to be done in your relationship to ensure the relationship is the reflection of the multiplication of the better.

Transparent Talk

We arrived at our next place. We had gotten to the point where we had learned how to become nurturing new vessels, and the essential part in this place is just learning how to be transparent and true. You may ask, "What does that mean?" Due to transparency and truth, today's message is not yesterday's message. Yesterday I felt a certain way about speaking up in our relationships, so people do not take things for granted. Do you need to speak up in spaces so you do not become stagnant or withdrawn from each other? Allowing the absence of your genuine feedback or feelings can cause regret that results in your relationship being pulled in the opposite direction of your true desires and purpose. This action transpires because of not speaking up. It is not because our mate does not want to understand our space. In addition, they want to nurture, and unfortunately, they become unsure how to be supportive in the silence. In our relationship, that is critical when we have something that ruffles our feathers or sets us back. We speak up and have hard conversations by choosing the correct words to convey our feelings. When we cautiously speak up, we are not being bold, brash, and careless with our conversation. Cautiously speaking up ensures that we do not create damage to our relationship. When you speak up, take the time to speak up in a way that can bring a positive change. Do not wait until issues have been suppressed and you speak up in an argument. Do not wait to speak up when things are just wrong. Speak up at the moment when you know that something has caused that pause, so it does not create a pause in your relationship. Spend your relationship going forward. If not, you will pay for it at the pauses or the moments that were never resolved. This is where we encourage you to focus on the forward progress of the now and the later. Now and later are very important in your relationship. Additionally, how you prepare each day to become a better version of yourself, to be a better we, to be a better unit, is just as important.

We leave you with three steps that have helped us get to a better we that we incorporate daily.

1. We have learned how to bring what we need to be in the space to become new vessels.

2. We have learned how to nurture each other.

3. We have learned how to speak up because silence can kill us.

Questions

Are you able to flow in faith and believe that GOD will work it out for your good?

Chapter 15

The Patience of A Married Couple Becoming One Flesh!

By
Contributing Authors
Jason and Rhonda Turner "The Turners"

"Even so, faith, if it hath not works, is dead, being alone. A man may say, Thou hast faith, and I have works: shew me thy faith without thy works, and I will shew thee my faith by my works."
James 2:17-18, KJV
#Patience
Bible Couple ~ Xerxes and Esther

W hat does becoming one flesh mean to you? Matthew 19:5-6 (ESV) says, "and said 'Therefore a man shall leave his father and his mother and hold fast to his wife, and the two shall become one flesh?' So they are no longer two but one flesh. What therefore God has joined together let not man separate." We come before you as a married couple, "one flesh" that grew to have grace, mercy, and patience during our marriage. Let us introduce ourselves, Jason Turner and Rhonda Turner, and we are "The Turners." We have been married 24 years and counting. God has taken care of us through our amazing journey that we call love. We, "The Turners," are pleased to be able to come to you and so many other married couples to share our story. We hope we will help another amazing couple in the world that may not believe that they are amazing and do not understand that God gives us grace, mercy, and, most importantly, patience.

After some real conversation and thought, my wife and I decided the couple from the Bible we identify ourselves with is Xerxes and Esther. They are suitable with our struggles and the commitment that gave us the strength to continue our marriage. Xerxes and Esther relate to us because of their marriage's love, grace, favor, and patience. Furthermore, their willingness to give back to the community while giving back to each other exhibits great strength. We identified with this and were able to relate and apply ourselves. We realized later in our marriage that life is what you make it. Sometimes it is easy to move in accordance with each other and occasionally challenging. However, we understand as an individual that it takes work from both parties. Every marriage has rough and difficult spots. Nevertheless, the question is, how do you face the challenges? In our story, we will try to give you some examples. Who said marriage is easy? Not us. After being married for 24 years, we would never tell anyone that if you do not have a perfect marriage, it would not work. God created conditions for humans in relationships. He also understood that our human nature sometimes makes this process difficult.

So let us move on with the history of "The Turners." We have been married for 24 years. We met in our 20s and began to take things seriously after a year of dating. At the beginning of our journey, we had many different challenges. We came into our relationship with our own baggage. I, Mrs. Turner, was in a previous relationship. I started having children at 18, and was in a mentally and physically abusive relationship before meeting my husband. He had a history of deviance with the law and legal issues and dated many other women at the same time.

Go figure. In the beginning, things that could go wrong went wrong within the relationship. We decided to push forward with the relationship. We persevered. We decided to get married and do our best to make this marriage work. Remember what we said earlier: marriage takes work, and we decided to WORK! Here we are, 24 years later, in a marriage where we are happier than ever. We had to work to get to know each other by communicating and learning our love languages. As the wife, we had challenges because of infidelity while dating. Trusting was not easy, but I decided to try. Mr. Turner was ready to make the change in my life because he knew I was the one he needed in his life. Therefore, whatever was not good for him, he had to let it go and work with what God gave him. When we decided to get married, the trust was not there, but we moved forward anyway with the marriage, BUT GOD! The first week after getting married, I was still hurting from the infidelity and requested to see the Pastor who married us. The Pastor did not understand why we had just now decided to let the cat out of the bag because I felt it was difficult to speak about the situation. Day in and day out, trying to mend that broken heart became very hard. It was difficult, but I started believing in the word that God says in James 2:17-18. "Even so, faith, if it hath not works, is dead, being alone. Yea, a man may say, thou hast faith, and I have works: shew me thy faith without thy works, and I will shew thee my faith by my works" (James 2:17-18, KJV).

I realized I could not want a change if I did not put in the work. My husband committed to me, and whatever it took, he tried to make it happen, rebuilding the trust needed in our marriage. We all make mistakes in life, but the question is, do we learn from the mistakes we make? What does it take to learn from the mistakes that we make? I often thought that God was a forgiving God. What makes me better as his wife? Why can't I forgive him and move forward? Was I the perfect one in this relationship? Did I deserve to be hurt? Does he deserve grace? There it is again. Human nature makes you believe that you are perfect and not mindful that we all make mistakes and deserve grace. Whereas God would have anything he puts together, let no man put it asunder.

Many of our friends (especially my wife's friend) did not agree with our relationship. This was due to her telling things we went through in our relationship. My wife felt that is what friends are for, right. No. We know some people are in your life for a reason—however, most of all, for a season. Many people did not think we would make it because of the vast differences in our backgrounds and how we entered our relationship. Where we are today, we understand God created this path for us. Regardless of what others may have thought, which is the important part.

One thing we recognized is that we came from two different cities in Florida. Her father and my uncle were Ministers, and they had known each other for many years. We never met until my wife relocated to a city closer to mine and began discussing family. We took a chance on one another and came into this union. We were young and ambitious but willing to show each other grace and patience. We know now that it would take time to build this thing that we call love.

I appreciate my husband. He stated that he was ready and proved that he was prepared to be my husband.

With many prayers and our commitment to each other, we recognized we had more in common than just our love for each other. As stated before, my wife was raised by her grandparents (mom). Her grandfather (father) was a Minister, so she was no stranger to God's word or working hard in the church or the community. This is where it all happened for my wife. When she was old enough to be on her own, she felt she wanted to save the world by helping youth and families. She did not want young people to make the same mistakes she did by getting pregnant at 17. Parents often say their children do not do bad things, but parents do not have honest conversations with their children about why they should not do those things. My wife says that is what happened to her. There was no discussion regarding sex, friendship, or relationships. It was all about church. I am not criticizing the church. My wife understood not everyone attends church. Most of the time, your children will start hanging out with someone that does not know God.

As the wife, I wanted to reach as many youths as possible, trying to save the world one child at a time. My husband saw my love for the youth and began to help me work in our community, but most of all, the work God intended for us to do.

I started by building community programs for youth, such as an award-winning girl's step team. The team won many competitions, but that was not my goal. The goal was to get them involved in something they like to do. They participated in positive workshops and completed community projects such as visiting nursing homes, talking with the elderly, and community clean-up day.

Due to a need in the community for boys, I created a basketball program. My husband and another outstanding coach were chosen to lead the basketball program. This was different. Our community had many basketball programs. They would not take the young men they thought were the worst of the crop. We took these young men and molded them into the men they are today. It is important to understand that we may not be able to save them all, but if we can make a difference in one, we are happy. Now we are not going to say it was easy. It was a challenge initially, but things started getting better when they realized someone cared. These young people came because of our hearts. Even though we chastised them, they realized later that it was needed. We were doing this daily. We would get phone calls from parents in the middle of the night to assist with a situation with their child in the home. Parents trusted us and knew we had good intentions. We lose children every day. Whatever we could do to help or save a young person's life, we were there.

Our boys played sports but still had a jealous spirit of others in their space. We did not realize until they were grown and able to express themselves. We tried to keep them active but to see others call us their parents hit them as they got older and wondered why they had to share their time with outside teens. It brought many teens into my home who were going through different situations. We are always willing to help the community's youth in any way we can.

In saving the world, it was many hours that my wife had to put into the youth and community. She had the mindset that she needed to work harder to change the mindset of the youth and adults. She would put in over 60 hours a week from 8 AM until 11 PM at her job, where she created events and programs. This consumed her time and the time she could have spent with the children and me. I had to talk with her about her time away from home and not fulfilling her husband's needs. She did not realize that she lost sight of her responsibility at home when she spent so much time doing other things. One of the best things she felt she could have done was to leave that job. Even though she loved the job, she realized it took away so much time from her family. When she left the job, I left coaching the basketball program my wife built from scratch because our time was being pulled in many different directions. So, do you think things slowed down at that time? No. My wife completed her Master's Degree in Mental Health and Marriage and Family, and I took classes with her to work with couples. Well, while in the Master's Degree program, we decided to open an event hall where people can come and rent the facility for special events. That was another mistake, but we learn from our mistakes, right.

We concluded that the benefits of the event hall were not worth the hassle. People wanted to rent it at a lower rate, and others thought we were the maintenance people. We even had some interested renters not return once they discovered we were the owners. The day we decided to close the event hall, my wife's mother (grandmother) passed away the next day. The death of her grandmother (mom) broke her heart. She was the family's glue and prayer warrior at that time. For 14 years, we cared for her. She taught us so many valuable lessons about having patience with one another. Shortly afterward, my wife decided to join Delta Sigma Theta Sorority, the Crimson and Cream, representing courage and purity. There was her time again. She could not be still, but I had the patience to let her do her desired things.

In 2010 my wife started a nonprofit called 4 Knowledge Is Power, where we take teens in grades 8 to 12 worldwide on college and historical tours. The students would never have an opportunity to experience college or learn about their history if 4 Knowledge Is Power did not exist. My wife and I worked together to plan and lead the tours. We call it teamwork, which makes our dream goal work.

Yet again, my wife took on another endeavor. She joined the National Coalition of 100 Black Women after being told she could bring the chapter to another level. She did just that, and it has consumed her time since 2013. She was asked to be Vice President of Membership. A question arose, "Where does all the work begin for her?" She replied, "The real work begins for me, but my husband is a champ and my biggest supporter."

My husband always made me feel like I could walk on the moon without a problem. He is always saying you can do it. I will always love him because it is easy to doubt yourself and say what you cannot do instead of saying, "I can do all things through Christ who strengthens me" (Philippians 4:13, NKJV). Years later, I was summoned to become the President of the Chapter. During my tenure as President, my husband was always there. He encouraged me and said, "Baby, you can do it." At that moment, I wrote up my plan to help black women all over connect with other black women in business. The group is called Black Women Business Connect (BWBC).

Today we live life with the express purpose of utilizing every second, minute, and hour to impact the lives of each other, the community, or the people who cross our path. With God's grace and favor, He built us for these times. Our patience for each other helped build our marriage for 24 years. We could not see it 25 years ago. However, it is clearer because there is a purpose. He has work for us to do. We learned how to trust in God and not our own understanding. We learned if we fall, we have the grace to get back up, and try again, but keep God in it. My husband prays daily for our marriage and family, encouraging me to do the same thing. He does not leave home until he prays and keeps us covered.

Happiness at this age is important in our lives. After years of communicating and learning from one another, we can say thank you, Lord, for giving us the patience to endure the obstacles and teaching us how to become one. The Cord of Three Strands symbolizes the joining of one man and one woman by God into a marriage relationship. Marriage takes three; you, your spouse, and God. God taught us to love by keeping him at the center of our marriage. His love will continue to bind us together as one. We thank God for this union!

We will continue to stand on the principle of patience, which allows you to be yourself and understand there will be mistakes. Patience allows for grace and communication. We will be able to achieve our ultimate goal of having a successful marriage.

Question

What does becoming one flesh mean to you?

Conclusion

Our prayer is that this book presented some answers to your most pressing questions. We pray that the Holy Spirit spoke to you and provided you comfort and peace that He has your marriage covered. We pray that the couples in this book helped to lighten your load through their story. We pray that your marriage is blessed beyond your wildest dreams!

Learn from these stories. Do not take anything for granted. Seek help when you need it. Do not be afraid to discuss the tough topics with your mate. One thing we have learned for sure is that "Communication" is the key. Every single situation in this book was solved using prayer and communication.

[Communication – imparting or exchanging of information or news between individuals through a common system of symbols, signs, or behaviors. Verbal or Written. The act of sending, sharing, or receiving information (talking, writing, listening, or reading).]

Impart into your mate. Share your deepest thoughts, dreams, aspirations, and goals. Listen to receive and speak to be understood. Allow your mate space to be transparent. Good communicators listen carefully, speak or write clearly, and respect different opinions.

True love:

1 Corinthians 13: 3-8 (NIV)

[3] If I give all I possess to the poor and give over my body to hardship that I may boast, but do not have love, I gain nothing.

[4] Love is patient, love is kind. It does not envy, it does not boast, it is not proud.

[5] It does not dishonor others, it is not self-seeking, it is not easily angered, it keeps no record of wrongs.

[6] Love does not delight in evil but rejoices with the truth.

[7] It always protects, always trusts, always hopes, always perseveres.

[8] Love never fails. But where there are prophecies, they will cease; where there are tongues, they will be stilled; where there is knowledge, it will pass away.

Grab the workbook that accompanies this book and start a group session to discuss and grow your relationship.

And remember..."If you build it, it will last!!!"

James and Cynthia

Afterword

I believe that James and Cynthia's vision to formulate this book to assist, encourage, and inspire couples to stay together in their marriage and make it great was truly Heaven sent and Heaven ordained by God. Especially during these challenging times.

All the stories that were shared will not only help marriages today but also for many years to come. I say this because, as a Pastor, my husband and I have seen more couples end in divorce or separation over the last two years, or should I say since the pandemic, than we have in all of our years of ministry. To be quite honest, even our marriage experienced tumultuous moments, more than ever, during this COVID-19 season, such as the inability to:

- Communicate effectively
- Resolve conflict
- Let go of the negative beliefs we both held in our minds toward one another.

The challenges we experienced in our marriage during the pandemic became so overwhelming. At times, the thought entered our minds to throw in the towel and quit. This was probably the worst season of our marriage ever, but thanks be to God, we decided to hang in there and give our marriage a chance it deserved. As a result, things started turning back around for the good.

We both decided to remain resilient to our vows and do whatever was necessary to place our marriage back on track to be full of fun, faith and make it great!

Now during those rocky moments, it was not always easy staying together, but we applied the following:

- We stayed connected to God and kept Him first.
- We read books similar to the one you are holding right now.
- We worked on ourselves and not each other.
- We communicated with one another by listening more than speaking.
- We were willing to apologize when we were wrong.
- We spent quality time with each other.

All of these focused actions assisted us in navigating through challenging, tough times and crossing the other side's threshold.

Therefore, whatever you are going through, keep reading this book and its victorious stories as often as necessary. If you can, attend all of James and Cynthia's marriage events. Do not give up on your marriage or each other because things can and will turn around if you persevere. Be resilient and apply all the information you have just read to your marriage. I promise you that you will not regret doing so.

Pastors Steve and Wanda Martin,
Higher Ground Church International
Philadelphia, Pennsylvania

Notes...

Notes...

Notes...

Notes...

_____

_____

_____

_____

_____

_____

_____

_____

_____

_____

_____

_____

_____

_____

_____

_____

_____

_____

_____

_____

_____

_____

_____

_____

_____

About the Authors

Louis and Tonia Bailey, Fayetteville, North Carolina

Louis and Tonia Bailey's love story started with an unplanned house visit with friends in April 1987 in Killeen, TX. Their married story began 34 years ago on April 9, 1988 (yes, they engaged and married in less than 12 months). Fast forward to two children and seven military relocations later, they are still committed to "Always" (Atlantic Starr, our wedding song). Has it always been easy? NO, but their love commitment is strong, standing through it all.

Free Gift: Date Night Game
Pt. 1: https://bit.ly/datenightgame1
Pt.2: https://bit.ly/datenightgamept2

Contact Info:
Website: www.hopeservicepllc.com
Email: tbailey@hopepllc.com

Eric and Placida Braswell, Marietta, Georgia

J. Eric Braswell has 30 years of ministry experience, including 19 years of training and equipping leaders for ministry and service to the community. Currently, Eric serves the community daily in his role at the mental health and human services organization as a trainer and consultant. He is experienced in training individuals, couples, and families with concepts and skills that produce wholeness and connection in their relationships. He is an Ordained Pastor, Pre-Marriage/Marriage & Parent Coach,

Family Coach, Certified Emotional Intelligence Coach, and Certified Cognitive Behavior Treatment Coach.

Placida Braswell has 20-plus years of leadership in ministry and the marketplace. She is the Founder and Chief Elevating Officer of Women Elevated, Inc., an organization to celebrate, empower and equip women for their purpose. She is an Ordained Pastor, Regional Program Director for a faith-based mental health and human services organization, and a Contributing Author to two book projects: *Dear Daughter* (2017) and *My Son* (2021). She obtained her Master's of Arts Degree in Human Services focused on Marriage and Family from Liberty University.

Free Gift: https://bit.ly/braswellness to schedule your free 30-minute session.

Contact Info:
Website: www.braswellgroup.com

Eric and Cassandra Ferguson, Churchville, Maryland

Tony and Cassandra have been married for 35 years. They have four children Chantre', Shaneka, Antonio Jr., and Antwan. One daughter in love, Renarda, and one son-in-love, Devin. Their world really changed when God blessed them with two beautiful granddaughters, Leonna and Amira. Tony and Cassandra have counseled, taught marriage Bible studies, led cell groups, mentored, and prayed for many couples for over 20 years. Their passion is to walk truthfully in their marriage and be an example for all generations. They currently serve as Deacon Care and Marriage Ministry leaders at Mount Pleasant Church and Ministries, where they have been attending for over 20 years.

Free Gift: In studio time for coaching and a PDF workbook on having victory in your finances.

Contact Info:
Elevation Global Media Group
Phone: 1-443-307-1241
Email: info@elevationglobalmediagroup.com

Darrell and Lisa Fiddermon, Fort Washington, Maryland

Darrel Fiddermon is a husband, father, coach, and Preacher. He leads a Sports Ministry with the Youth Athlete University (formerly known as the PG Bears). This faith-based nonprofit organization uses sports to build character and grow Christian leaders. For many years, he has been promoting the link between sports and faith as an outreach for the gospel of Jesus. He has now become a well-known and respected coach and mentor to other coaches, families, and youth across the DMV area. You can learn more about this ministry at www.youthathleteuniverstiy.org.

Dr. Lisa M. Fiddermon is a wife, mother, entrepreneur, Preacher, speaker, and author. She is also the Owner/Founder of Love with Finesse LLC. Love with Finesse LLC, helps individuals who struggle with faith and mental health crises find healing and embrace wellness so they can fully enjoy their relationships. She earned two degrees from Wesley Theological Seminary with an MDiv. and a DMin in Pastoral Psychotherapy. While serving as a Lead Pastor for ten years, she was introduced to people of faith who were secretly struggling with faith and mental health issues. She realized she was not doing enough to help people of faith to find healing and wellness in trauma, depression, and anxiety. So, she started a business built on The Great Commandment of Jesus to "love with all our mind, heart, and soul." It is a business that provides a ministry of care to such individuals.

Free Gift: Email LoveWithFinesse@gmail.com to receive your eGift with the tagline "MMG-Gift".

Contact Info:
Website: LoveWithFinesse@gmail.com

Emilio and Sharon Grant, Peachtree City, Georgia

Emilio and Sharon have been married for 14 years. They use their lived marital experience with the Prepare-Enrich Couple Assessment and Skill-Building to coach married couples in fostering healthy relationships and marriage longevity. Emilio and Sharon each know how challenging married life can be when you do not have the emotional bandwidth to handle life's stressors properly, directly impacting your overall satisfaction in marriage.

Free Gift: Couple Connect 30-Day Calendar
https://bit.ly/3POh2yv

Contact Info:
Website: www.oasisofserenity.net

William and Tasheka Green, Upper Marlboro, Maryland

Dr. Tasheka L. Green is a transformational servant leader who leads with the heart of a servant but the mind of a leader. Dr. Green is a transformational coach, influential educator, inspirational speaker, best-selling author, entrepreneur, philanthropist, and 2022 Maryland American Mother, Inc. of the Year. Dr. Green is the President, Founder, and Chief Executive Officer of To Everything There Is a Season, Inc. They provide personal, professional, leadership, and educational coaching and consulting to help individuals and organizations maximize their greatest potential. Dr. Green is featured in the Harvard University School of Education, HarvardX Course, Introduction to Data Wise: A Collaborative Process to Improve Learning & Teaching for her innovative coaching approaches to employ the Data Wise Improvement Process to impact systemic change within an organization. Because of her competency in bringing coherence to improving culture, systems, structures, and people, Dr. Green is sought after by many. Dr. Green is committed to the calling of serving and leading others. She works tirelessly to ensure that everyone she meets reaches his or her maximum potential. This extensive background has allowed her to touch and inspire many lives.

William Z. Green Sr. is a God-fearing man who loves God and his family. Born and raised in Washington, District of Columbia, and the Maryland Metropolitan Area, William Z. Green Sr. learned how to overcome life's challenges and press towards a place called promise. William Z. Green Sr. graduated from Eleanor Roosevelt High School in Greenbelt, Maryland, and attended Sojourner Douglass College in Baltimore, Maryland. William Z. Green Sr. is the Vice-President of *To Everything There is a Season: The*

Deborah C. Offer Bulgin Memorial Foundation, Incorporated, "leading people to their dreams and visions by providing them with support to help them attain their hearts' desires." William is the Proprietary and Chief Operating Officer of *Signature by William Green,* which specializes in customized services to your needs. William Z. Green Sr. is a true worshiper who radiates the love and joy of the Lord. He is a member of The Gathering in Forestville, MD, serving as a Deacon under the leadership of the Honorable Bishop Donald A. Wright, Pastor, and Lady Dr. Nakia Wright.

William Sr. and Dr. Tasheka L. Green have three beautiful children: Marquis (25), Mikayla (12), and William Jr. (9).

Free Gift: Visit www.2eseasons.com and subscribe to our website to receive our weekly words of inspiration, hope, and a free gift

Contact Info:
Website: www.2eseasons.com

James and Cynthia Greene, Waldorf, Maryland

James and Cynthia Greene are Founders of Marriage Built 2 Last, LLC. They are Marriage and Relationship Visionary Strategists and Ordained Ministers. They help couples see what God sees for them by assisting couples to create vision and goals for their marriage so they can achieve all He has for them to do and have! Their goal is to help eradicate divorce, chaos, and confusion in marriages by providing couples with a purpose that builds marriages that last and fulfill their dreams and destiny.

James and Cynthia are 2x Best Seller Authors of *Don't Get Married If…. And 40 Day Journey to the #MarriageOfYourDreams.* They are passionate & prolific Speakers, Certified Professional Relationship Coaches, and Prepare & Enrich Certified. They provide online courses, workshops, retreats, and conferences and have the #1 Couples Membership Club: The In Love and Loving It Couples Academy. They have been married for 15 years. They have four amazing adult children, Antwine, Natasha, Andrew, Kathryn and a German Shepherd named Noa Grace. They are Deacons at Victory Christian Ministries International, where the Pastors are Apostles Tony and Cynthia Brazelton. They serve as Marriage Counselors, are in the Drama Ministry, the Prime Tyme Choir, and often serve in Children's Church. They led the Marriage ministry for over four years. Their favorite past times are traveling, power walking, worship, and spending all of their time with each other and family.

Free Gift: Get your free 17 Ways to Kiss Challenge List, https://bit.ly/kissinglist

Contact Info:
Website: www.marriagebuilt2last.com
Email: info@marriagebuilt2last.com

Meechie Jefferis, Greenbelt, Maryland

Demetrica "Meechie" Jefferis is a Chicago native, retired Air Force Veteran, eight-year plus Breast Cancer Thriver, and author of *No More Bad Days.* Since Sept 2018, she has served as a licensed Financial Professional and Financial Literacy Educator. With three plus years of experience, she has educated and empowered more than 500 families, and secured $20M in financial assets for those seeking to build financial stability and independence.

Free Gift: Please contact Meechie Jefferis at

meechiejefferis@gmail.com for your free book *Saving Your Future/Finance 101*, along with a free financial review.

Contact Info:
Email: meechiejefferis@gmail.com
Phone: 1-240-210-4489

Dexter and Philomena Johnson,

Middleburg Heights, Ohio

Dr. Dexter Johnson is an Aerospace Pioneer, Chief Reconciliation Ambassador, Excellence and Leadership Cultivator, and a Certified Marriage and Relationship Facilitator.

Dr. Philomena M. Johnson is Chief Education and Relationship Empowerment Strategist; Leadership, Policy, and Change in Education, Oxford Women's Roundtable Presenter, Certified Marriage and Relationship Facilitator.

Free Gift: Receive a complimentary 30-minute brilliant relationship consultation when you connect with us at www.phidexenterprises.com.

Contact Info:
Website: www.phidexenterprises.com

Joel and Naomi Mitchell, Chicago, Illinois

Revs. Drs. Joel and Naomi Mitchell are the Co-Pastors of the Morgan Park Baptist Church of Chicago, Illinois. They also founded The Family and Marriage Institute of Chicago. This not-for-profit organization provides pastoral care and counseling to individuals and families. The Marriage Investors, LLC is a global ministry that provides pastoral care and coaching services for dating, engaged individuals, and married couples. Over their nineteen years as husband and wife, Joel and Naomi have developed a passion for individuals, married couples, and families who need to restore wholeness by healing brokenness. They are committed to reconciling relationships, deepening love, and securing familial bonds. They love God and consider God integral in their lives, marriage, and ministry.

Joel is an Ordained Minister and graduated in May of 2018 with a Doctor of Ministry in Pastoral Care and Counseling from the Chicago Theological Seminary. Naomi is a licensed Minister with a heart for wholeness and well-being. She earned her Doctor of Ministry in Homiletics in May of 2021 from the Association of Chicago Theological Schools. They are authors of the book *Shattered – How to Overcome a Broken Marriage*. They are the proud parents of three children, 18-year-old twin boys, Jasper Caleb and Jacobi Israel; a 16-year-old daughter, Sidni Joi and a seven-year-old Golden Retriever Maximillion Nicholas Mitchell.

Free Gift: Receive a free copy of our 10 commandments of Conversation guide. www.TheMarriageInvestors.com

Contact Info:
Website: www.TheMarriageInvestors.com
Email: contact@TheMarriageInvestors.com

William and Larrissa Parker, Brandywine, Maryland

William and Larrissa Parker met in England 21 years ago while serving on active-duty Air Force. They have been married since 2011 and reside in Brandywine, MD. They are a blended family in which they are the proud parents of four adult children and a very active nine-year-old. They will be the first to admit marriage can be challenging at times, but with God, as the Head, you can experience a marriage that fulfills all your heart's desires. William and Larrissa are both United States Air Force veterans after 24 years of service. They are also owners of Urban Expressionz LLC. They are laying the groundwork for establishing "Land of Eden, a place of refuge," a transitional housing unit for the homeless in Maryland.

Free Gift: Get 12 Date Ideas to Enhance Your Marriage - bit.ly/FriendshiponFire

Contact Info: Contact@urbanexpressionz.com

Rodney and Michele Peake, Odenton, Maryland

Michele and Rodney Peake are high school sweethearts married for over 29 years. Michele is a minister, certified Life Coach, producer, and 3X Bestselling author with over 25 years of leadership and training experience. Rodney is a Deacon, successful playwright, and Director. He is currently in minister's training and has enjoyed being a technician with a Fortune 500 company for over 20 years. They both have won several Public Speaking Awards with Toastmasters International. Under the leadership of Senior Pastor Charles E. Cato Sr., they serve on several ministries together at Mt. Calvary Baptist Church of

Lanham, MD. They have two beautiful daughters, Zarina and Nia, and one grandson, Zavala.

Free Gift: Receive a 30 minute Free Couple's Check-Up by sending an email to michele@michelereneeconsulting.com

Contact Info:
Website: www.michelereneeconsulting.com

Dwight and Deidra Roussaw, Nashville, Tennessee

Ministers Dwight and Deidra Roussaw married on August 8, 1998. They exemplify the portrait of a Christ-centered and Christian-based marriage. They are the proud parents of one daughter and the loving grandparents of four grandchildren and (a grand angel). They are licensed and Ordained Ministers, co-founders of TWOgether Marriages® and Kairi's Travel®, authors of *Marriage on Fire, The Marriage Make Over, From the Bedroom to the Boardroom, The Husbands Journey, The Wife's Journal and Date Night Coaching*, hosts of the Marriage on Fire Radio Show, monthly Date Night Tour and certified Sandals WeddingMoon Specialist and Cruise Specialist. In their Marriage on Fire Bible Fellowship, they host seminars for spouses by spouses and servant leaders of two: Be One Marriage Fellowship at The Resurrection Center under the leadership of Dr. S. Todd & Dr. Cleo V. Townsend, Bishop, and Pastor. Minister Deidra is a certified signature wife coach, certified leadership mentor, relationship and leadership expert, wife blogger, speaker, and the founder of TrulyWed Wives®, a wives leadership ministry offering wife coaching, wife mentoring, wives retreats, and conferences.

Free Gift: Download: Loving Your Spouse
Unconditionally, eBook, https://payhip.com/b/5xEf

Contact Info:
www.twogethermarriages.org,
info@twogethermarriages.org
Phone: 1-800-960-0098

Fulton and Cortne Smith, Winston, Georgia

Cortne' Lee Smith's love magnet drew in Fulton Smith. She married a widower, and he married a widow. She is a student of numbers, an instructor of law, and a woman that lives by love. She is a Relationship Coach & Grief Specialist who has gained the title of "The Love Lady." Fulton brought his experiences of a 32-year marriage to the station. Moreover, he brought his skills as a certified technician for over 30 plus years, 17 years of over-the-road hazmat driving. Together they champion their movement -To Be More Than Alive #Choose to L.I.V.E, by co-hosting "The Weekend Widow(er)s Word" via the Relationship Service Station YouTube channel and special radio broadcast for widows and widowers with Fulton. As life partners, they have developed curricula and lessons to empower the left behind to thrive, not just survive the loss of their life partner.

Contact Info:
Email: Cortne@relationshipservicestation.com
Phone: 1-678-718-5019

William and Rhonda Turner, Delray Beach, Florida

The Turners have been married for 24 plus years and they are getting ready to celebrate 25 years of love. Mr. Turner is a full-time local truck driver that does an amazing job of taking care of his family and being the head of his household. Mrs. Turner has been a role model, mentor, and community leader in her community for over 25 years. The Turners are the founders of 4 Knowledge is Power Inc. a Nonprofit.

They wanted to do more for their community to enhance the lives of married couples and started Marriage Counseling where they counsel couples together. Their goal is to help married couples have a chance to have a successful marriage, then the children could have a greater opportunity and the community will have better circumstances. They also became a Marriage Life Coach, Certified Relationship Workshop facilitators, and Life Coach to assist them with their journey to reach married couples. The Turners are on God's mission not their own and having the faith and patience to do the work of God is important to them. Turner's mottos are Dream Bigger, Reach Higher and Achieve More.

Free Gift: To get your free 30 minute consultation go to https://linktr.ee/turner_enterprise

Contact Info:
Website: https://linktr.ee/turner_enterprise

Literary Works

Other literary works by 2x Best Seller Authors James and Cynthia Greene

Visit our Author Page on Amazon:
https://www.amazon.com/author/cynthiawhitegreene

40 Day Journey to the #MarriageOfYourDreams

Imagine 40 days entirely spent in God's presence, and then imagine 40 days spent completely with your spouse. This 40-day journey to the marriage of your dreams takes you and your spouse on a spiritual journey with the two of you, plus your Spiritual Head. In this book, you get a plan that includes fasting, praying, scripture and devotion together. During this time, you will hear a word from God concerning your marriage and things to help you strengthen and grow the biblical foundation so you can enjoy marriage the way God intended you to and not the "world's" way.

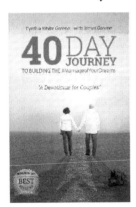

Don't Get Married If...

Don't Get Married If.... Is a provoking tool that promotes deep and sometimes difficult discussions about your dating life and future spouse. This book is designed to crystalize your thoughts and reflections to help root out issues, overcome barriers, break through past trauma and triggers, and develop a strategy for marital success. After reading this book, be prepared to take your relationship with the one you care about to a higher and deeper level. Be ready to have one of the best marriages that will last a lifetime because you took the time to have the 'tough' conversations before saying, "I Do."

Be sure to Get Your Free copy of Lessons Learned in *Love, Couples of the Bible Story Teaches Couples of Today*, only at

www.makemarriagesgreat.com

COUPLES
DETERMINED TO MAKE
MARRIAGE
GREAT

VISIONARY AUTHORS
JAMES AND CYNTHIA GREENE

Made in the USA
Middletown, DE
02 October 2022

11723987R00097